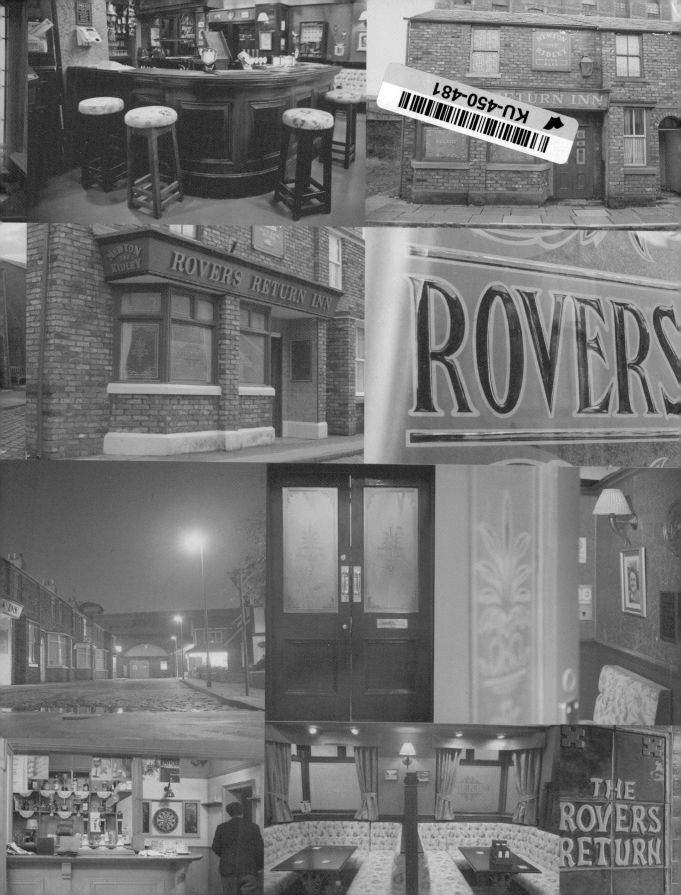

THE ROVERS RETURN

·CORONATION ST.· ™

OFFICIAL COMPANION

TIM RANDALL

headline

ITV STUDIOS
GLOBAL ENTERTAINMENT

This book is dedicated to the memory of Betty Driver.
The heart of the Rovers from 1969 to 2011.

Coronation Street is an ITV Studios Production
Copyright © ITV Studios Ltd 2013

The right of Tim Randall to be identified as the Author of
the Work has been asserted by him in accordance with the
Copyright, Designs and Patents Act 1988.

First published in 2013
by HEADLINE PUBLISHING GROUP

1

Cataloguing in Publication Data is available from the British Library

Hardback ISBN 978 0 7553 6545 6
Trade paperback ISBN 978 0 7553 6547 0

Design by Perfect Bound Ltd
Picture Research by Dave Woodward
All images used courtesy of ITV Studios Ltd

Printed and bound in Italy by Rotolito Lombarda SpA

Headline's policy is to use papers that are natural, renewable and recyclable products and made from
wood grown in sustainable forests. The logging and manufacturing processes are expected to conform
to the environmental regulations of the country of origin.

HEADLINE PUBLISHING GROUP
An Hachette UK Company
338 Euston Road
London NW1 3BH

www.headline.co.uk
www.hachette.co.uk

The author would like to thank the cast and crew of Coronation Street.

Special thanks to Helen Nugent, Dominic Khouri, Emma Tait, Dan Newman, Kieran Roberts, Shirley
Patton, Jonathan Taylor, Sarah Moolla, Dave Woodward, Scarlett Taulbut, Kevin Morgan, Jo Baggott,
Stella Rigby, Vicky Johnson, Sam Walker, Richard Stevens, Katherine Brown, Alison Sinclair, Andy
Baker, David Crook, Wendy Granditer, Kate Davidson-Ashcroft, Iain McCallum, Jojo Dipple, Deirdre
O'Brien, Neill Ludmon, Tony Weber, Tony Wright, Keith Watson, Nellie Harvey and Mark Horner.

Contents

Introduction

As veteran barmaid Betty Williams once sagely noted, 'If you're not being talked about in this pub, you're not worth serving.' As ever, the Rovers' longest-serving employee was spot on. In Coronation Street's iconic watering hole no secret has been safe, no affair left unexposed. Friendships have been forged – and smashed – relationships have fizzled and scores have been summarily settled. (More often than not with a swift right hook or a pint unexpectedly hurled into the face.)

Whether it was barmaid Tina going into labour, Vera taking a swipe at Jack, Peter being unmasked as a bigamist, Bet's disastrous love life or even a one-off sighting of Norris in drag, for more than 50 years there's been plenty going on in the Rovers to keep the gossips entertained. 'Who needs the theatre?' sighed Blanche Hunt, after watching one such escapade unfold in front of her eyes as she sipped her (large) gin and tonic.

Change has never gone down a storm with the Rovers' regulars. All hell broke loose in 1967 when landlady Annie Walker tried to take the pub upmarket with a chic Parisienne theme. Six years later there was uproar when temporary manager Glyn Thomas installed a one-armed bandit and an organist. Forty years on and the resistance to change remains the same.

Gloria Price attempted to raise the tone for the Rovers' most recent grand reopening with a number of gastro-pub-style touches plus a newspaper rack on the side, but the clientele were simply relieved to see their beloved boozer restored to its former glory. And it was Betty's legendary hotpot not Gloria's scampi goujons that continued to fly out of the kitchen…

The very heart of Coronation Street, the Rovers is more than somewhere to just sup a pint – it's where the locals

Rita: *'Eee, when I think of the hours we've spent in here over the years…'*
Emily: *'It's a wonder they don't charge us rent.'*

come to celebrate and commiserate, to confront and to cogitate. And there, despite any unfolding drama in the back room, they are always guaranteed a warm welcome, a shoulder to cry on and the comforting waft of a hearty hotpot seeping through to the bar.

This book is a celebration of the Rovers and all who have swigged in her – so pull up a bar stool, get Liz McDonald to bring over your usual, and prepare to relive some of the Rovers Return's most memorable moments...

The Management

It takes a licensee with a rod of iron to run the Rovers – just ask any of the staff who have worked for them. Whether it was steely Annie Walker's determination to remain a cut above her clientele, firm but fair Bet's stony-faced glares that could freeze ice at fifty paces or Liz McDonald's attempts to hold the fort whilst managing the chaos of her own, and son Steve's, ever unfurling love lives. Each of them has helped turn the Rovers into the iconic ale house it is today...

The welcoming Walkers...

Just as newlyweds Jack Walker and Annie took over the Rovers Return, World War II broke out and Jack was called up to join the army. After seeing action in France with the Lancashire Fusiliers, all Jack wanted on his return home was a quiet life behind the bar of his beloved boozer. The same could not be said for his social-climbing wife Annie, a woman determined to make her way to the top. She never quite managed it, instead opting to rule regally over the Rovers Return in a manner more befitting a queen than a local landlady. 'I have been in the hub of the community,' she once mused. 'You might even say I have had my own little kingdom.'

Annie was intent on lifting the Rovers from a working man's alehouse to something much more sophisticated, and was forever trying to take the Weatherfield boozer upmarket. But whenever her grand plans spun out of control, which they often did, you could guarantee it was the easy-going Jack who would be at her side to calm down the situation. He would gently remind his haughty wife that, for all her airs and graces, she'd actually been working in a cotton mill when they'd first met.

▲ ▶ All smiles from the Walkers; but snooty Annie didn't always see the funny side of her regulars' antics.

In 1966 Annie found a grand oil painting of an aristocratic woman in the cellar and on later discovering the frame was stuffed with money and a mask, she became convinced the Rovers had an exotic and romantic past of historical importance. She approached the brewery and insisted the name of the pub should be changed to 'The Masked Lady' and turned into a tourist attraction. Needless to say, the locals held a meeting and swiftly called a halt to Annie's plans and the Rovers has remained the Rovers ever since.

Earlier that year Annie had decided that offering a cheeseboard to accompany the ales was a great idea to raise the pub's standards. However, the locals were so unimpressed it only lasted one day. Her attempt at a cocktail hour didn't fare much better either, when all the regulars deserted the Rovers for the Laughing Donkey. She told Hilda Ogden she'd abandon the sophistication of cocktails because it was like 'feeding strawberries to pigs', and her loyal cleaner couldn't help but agree.

'I have been in the hub of the community. You might even say I have had my own little kingdom.'

Annie

Another time she decided that what the pub really needed was a dress code to keep out the riff-raff. She snootily insisted she would only serve customers if they were smartly attired. This didn't go down well with mouthy machinist Ivy Tilsley when Annie refused to serve her mechanic son Brian in his oily overalls. In protest the regulars voted with their feet and headed for the Flying Horse. With takings down £15 Annie had no choice but to reverse the policy.

While you could guarantee the regulars would be the first to bring her down a peg or two whenever Annie got ideas above her station, they also held her in great affection. They once threw her a *This Is Your Life* surprise to show how much they cared about her. In 1973, when she toyed with the idea of leaving the pub in the hands of manager Glyn Thomas, grim-faced regular Ena Sharples – not a woman prone to sentimentality – started a petition appealing for her to reconsider. Within hours the petition had 47 names on it and when it was presented to the stunned landlady, she was so touched she agreed to stay. That same year she was in her element when she was made Lady Mayoress – finally she'd achieved an almost regal social standing – and handed the running of the pub to her unreliable son Billy.

Despite the high regard her customers had for her, Annie did on several occasions consider abandoning the backstreet alehouse for classier premises. In 1961 the brewery offered her and Jack the chance to move into the much grander Royal Oak in leafy Sharringley. Jack felt too old to move to another pub, but struggled to admit it when he saw how much Annie had fallen hook, line and sinker for the fitted carpets, large car park and shiny cocktail bar. However, despite all her snobbish tendencies, she did love Jack and could see he was only agreeing to the move for her sake, so they decided to stick with what they knew and stayed put.

In 1969 the Walkers finally agreed on a fresh start. It all began with the brewery's Perfect Landlady competition, during which Annie

◄ Annie holds court behind the bar as Jed, Ena and Hilda listen in.
▲ Ena lays down the law to Annie.
▼ Jack and Annie play host to Len, Swindley and Stan.

Annie's French Fancy

In 1967, after becoming Cutie-Beauty Cosmetics' 100,000th customer, Annie won a weekend in Paris with a handsome French film star. She brought back a beret for Jack, a French book for Lucille Hewitt and started driving everyone mad swooning to French records and preparing French meals. 'Wandering over a Seine bridge in the moonlight doesn't encourage one to think of *chez moi* or even of one's life partner,' she sighed when asked if she'd missed home. The regulars felt sorry for Jack, but enjoyed poking fun at Annie. 'I'm waiting for her to do a can-can,' giggled Irma. Such was her new-found passion for all things Parisienne that she even considered putting bistro tables outside the Rovers to create a café-style atmosphere. To make the point that this was Weatherfield not the Marais, Ken Barlow hatched a plan which soon put a stop to Annie's French fantasies by instructing the men to order their pints in wine glasses, which created so much extra work that Jack put his foot down and it was *au revoir* to Annie's Paris dreams.

drove the regulars mad with her out-of-character niceness, until Ray Langton finally spotted what was going on and offered to nominate her for the competition. In a bid to win she installed a suggestion box on the bar, covered the pub in old Lancashire memorabilia, including clogs and miners lamps, and even offered cleaner Hilda a pay rise to keep her on side. After days on tenterhooks she finally received a telegram telling her she'd won – she later framed the note and hung it up by the bar. The prize was a trip to Majorca and whilst out there she was offered the chance to run the brewery's latest pub there.

They had two weeks to decide before opting to take what could be their final chance to fulfil Annie's dream of going up in the world. But at the very last minute the brewery withdrew the offer, telling the disappointed Walkers they were too old for a trendy Majorca bar. The unflappable Annie refused to let the situation get her down and turned their leaving party into a bash to celebrate the fact they were staying.

► At first Annie took against new barmaid Betty, but the pair soon developed a mutual respect.

Life was to change dramatically for the landlady in 1970 when her cherished Jack died suddenly of a heart attack. She was utterly devastated but grateful for the support of her senior barmaid Betty Turpin and new girl Bet Lynch. Annie had initially disapproved of both of them for being a touch too common, but soon the unlikely trio became a winning team.

However, son Billy proved to be less useful, continuing with his wayward ventures, racking up huge gambling debts and even losing the takings several times during dodgy poker matches. Annie found herself alone when Billy moved to Jersey to work in a hotel and during this time was the victim of an armed robbery. Typically, Annie stood up to the pair who were ransacking her drawers and they eventually fled, running into neighbours Ray Langton and Len Fairclough who gave them a good beating. But the incident had frightened the ageing widow and the brewery decided she needed a male presence around the place, so she hired widower Fred Gee as a live-in cellar-man.

Meanwhile Annie continued in her lofty quest to take the Rovers upmarket – but as ever her efforts saw her brought back down to earth with a bump. When Eddie Yeats tried to get her interested

ROVERS RETURN
Surprise, Surprise!

Annie seemed to be speechless when the regulars threw a surprise party to celebrate her 40 years at the Rovers' helm, but Bet had an inkling she'd known about it all along, as she just happened to be wearing her very best party frock. 'I think I know what you're suspecting,' Annie responded, enigmatically. 'But you see, dear, after 40 years on these premises there is nothing, absolutely nothing, that escapes my notice.'

in a new carpet for the back room she gave him short shrift. 'Mr Yeats, now how can I say this without sounding too insulting? I wouldn't trust you as far as I could throw a hogshead of bitter.' But her interest was piqued when he told her the carpet would be personalised and monogrammed in pure gold with an interlocking A and W. She paid £71 for it to be laid and threw a sherry morning for the Lady Victuallers to show off the carpet in all its glory. But just as the first guests were arriving Bet broke it to her that the carpet was actually from the trashy Alhambra Weatherfield Bingo Hall, which had just had a refurbishment. Aghast, Annie had to grin and bear it until she collared Eddie Yeats and demanded a refund.

In 1980 she embarked on another ambitious plan to extend the food menu. Annie started selling soup and sandwiches and agreed to give the staff a pay rise, installing a little bell to be rung when the food was ready to be served. Perched on a stool by the optics she enjoyed ringing the bell – once for Betty,

'She really believes that there's her and the rest of us. She's not being condescending or 'owt. She really believes it.'

Bet on Annie

◀ Annie shows Bet the secret to correctly pouring a sweet sherry.
▲ Lonely Annie takes a trip down memory lane on her wedding anniversary.

'Does her name sound as though it ought to be over a pawnshop or is it just that I'm prejudiced?'

Annie on Bet

twice for Bet and three times for Fred. This didn't go down well with the staff and once again the gimmick was short-lived.

But although Annie liked to put on a high and mighty facade, her life did have its disappointments. While she was proud of her daughter Joan, who lived in a well-to-do area of Derby, it became clear that Joan considered herself to be a cut above her mother. Not only did she believe Weatherfield was beneath her, she never deigned to visit the Rovers. Meanwhile the irresponsible Billy constantly rebelled against his mother's expectations and continued to let her down.

In 1984 Annie retired from the pub and went to stay with Joan in Derby, leaving Billy in charge. While he'd initially shown little interest in taking on the tenancy, he was eventually persuaded when Annie offered to pay off his gambling debts and keep the Rovers Return as a family business.

◄ The landlady poses in the pub for one last time.
▼ A big hug for Annie from beloved son Billy.
► Billy's stint running the Rovers fails to impress barmaids Bet and Betty.

It was to be a short-lived tenancy and his name was above the door for less than a year. During this ill-fated time he crossed the brewery on several occasions and also had numerous brushes with the law, thanks to his illegal lock-ins and illicit gambling sessions. He also fell out with Annie's loyal staff and sacked Fred, which left Bet and Betty fearful for the future of the pub and their jobs. The end

Food for Thought

In a bid to impress the brewery, temporary manager Fred Gee decided to lay on hot pies at lunchtime, hoping journalist Ken Barlow would give the pub a glowing review in the *Weatherfield Recorder*'s weekly dining-out column, 'Food For Thought'.

Unfortunately for Fred – and much to Bet and Betty's amusement – the portly pot-man doubled up in pain after eating one of his own bargain-basement pies (it later turned out he was suffering from appendicitis) and Ken wasn't impressed either. He complimented Bet and Betty's 'sparkling service which, along with the excellent ales, went some way to compensate for the quality of the food, which alas is well below the standard expected of pub grub in these days of the bistro explosion.'

came when the pub was raided by police in a tip-off about after-hours drinking. Newton & Ridley threatened him with eviction when they discovered he had been stocking the bar with non-brewery liquor for his own profit.

Billy handed back the tenancy before the brewery could take him to court and the much-disliked relief manager Gordon Lewis stepped in to hold the fort. Betty, who took against him in particular, urged Bet to apply for the permanent manager's role and another Rovers' era was about to begin…

► Bet celebrates having
her name over the door.
▼ The new landlady
poses with barmaids
Gloria and Sally.
► Festive fun for Bet,
Alec and the regulars.

Bet gets the top job...

No-nonsense Bet knew the pub trade inside-out and ran the Rovers in a way that would have made Mrs Walker proud. But no one could have been prouder of Bet than she was of herself. She couldn't believe after all the knocks and setbacks she'd had in life, she'd finally made something of herself and had got her name over the door of an establishment like the Rovers. This was the one place she'd been able to call home and by the time Bet took over, she'd become as much a part of the Rovers as the pumps themselves.

In 1987 the brewery decided they no longer wanted a manageress in the pub, but wanted to let the Rovers as a tenancy in order to boost profits. So Bet either had to buy it or move out. She told them she wanted first refusal but was shocked when they asked

'Well it's a rough old pub and it needs a rough old bird to keep charge of it!'
Mike on Bet

'I was pulling pints before I was legally old enough to drink 'em… There's not a lot I don't know about pubs. And even less I don't know about customers.'

Bet

for £15,000. She only had £3,000 in savings and realised once she had made her loan repayments, she wouldn't have any money to live on. In desperation, she turned to her friend and sparring partner, the crafty Alec Gilroy, a former showbiz agent who now ran the rival Graffiti Club. As a man known for his tight-fisted nature it came as something as a shock when Alec agreed to loan her the money, but then he'd always had his eye on Bet and the Rovers.

After just two months Bet struggled to cope with the repayments and when profits failed to improve, she feared she was in danger of losing her much-loved pub again. Her solution was to disappear overnight. Alec contacted the brewery and in an effort to protect his investment, suggested they allow him to take over as temporary manager.

◄ Newlyweds Bet and Alec balance the books.

Eventually Bet contacted the brewery to tell them she was in Spain and on hearing of her whereabouts, Alec hopped on the first flight out. He finally tracked her down to a grotty bar and was stunned to find her waiting on tables – but not as stunned as Bet was at being found. She admitted she couldn't cope with the finances and had been too ashamed to ask him for help. She insisted that although she was boracic, he could have his money back as soon as she'd signed the tenancy over. But Bet was even more surprised when Alec suggested there was another way she could return to running the Rovers – if she married him.

The odd couple tied the knot at All Saints Church in September 1987 to the surprise of almost everyone that knew them – and maybe themselves as well. They even found time to snarl at each other during their vows when Alec accused Bet of having an affair with pot-man Jack Duckworth. Bet was delighted, though, when Alec gave her the Rovers' tenancy as a wedding present. While there was no doubt they were an unlikely pairing, with slimy Alec more concerned with the takings than the needs of his wife, their relationship of bickering and bantering seemed to work.

Shortly after their marriage Bet discovered she was pregnant and even Alec was taken aback at how excited he was at the prospect of them having a child together. But their happiness was short-lived when Bet miscarried. The tragic event was particularly tough for Bet

'Where I went wrong was going into the licensed trade in the first place. Tropical fish, that was my other idea.'
Alec

RIDLEY'S AMERICAN DREAM

When new brewery upstart Nigel Ridley announced he was planning a trendier image for the Rovers, it didn't go down well with Bet or Alec. The premises were to be renamed Yankees and the ambitious plans included buying the Barlows' next door and turning the upper floor into a restaurant called the Bronx Bar. He even wanted the staff to wear uniforms and baseball caps. Instead the Gilroys went on strike, barricading themselves into the Rovers and only serving trusted regulars via the backyard. Luckily for the locals, when Ridley attempted to repossess the pub, former brewery grandee Cecil Newton came out of retirement and turned on him, dismissing his 'foolish young ideas' and declaring: 'Nobody is going to be wearing cowboy hats and selling fire water in the Rovers while I'm alive. The Rovers stays as it is, a working men's pub where working men live.'

'If Nigel flaming Ridley thinks he can get me running a pub where they'd reckon I was dressed posh wearing a boiler suit with more than one zip – he's got another thing coming!'

Bet

as it sharply brought back the pain and despair she'd experienced in 1975 when her only child, Martin, who she'd given up for adoption as a baby, was killed in a car crash.

While losing their unborn baby did momentarily bring the Gilroys closer together, their marriage came to an end in 1992 when Alec was offered the job of a lifetime as Entertainments Manager at Sunliners Cruise Line based in Southampton. It was his dream job and although Bet could see how much it meant to him, she couldn't face leaving her friends and her home. After talking it over with Betty she became nostalgic about the past and when Alec accepted a low valuation on the pub, telling her money didn't matter, she realised she belonged in the

Rovers and couldn't leave. She asked him to stay in Weatherfield with her, but a furious Alec accused Bet of always putting the pub first, and in doing so this time she had wrecked their marriage. With those parting words he left for Southampton, leaving behind a heartbroken Bet.

Once more she picked herself up, dusted herself down and painted on a smile for the punters out front. Soon, profit-obsessed Newton & Ridley boss Richard Willmore was on her case and informed her she was overstaffed. He demanded she let someone go but Bet insisted she'd checked the accounts and refused to sack anyone.

However, when Willmore went through the books with her Bet discovered Alec had been claiming wages for both Hilda Ogden, who'd retired six years earlier, and long-gone former barmaid Angie Freeman, and had thereby been fiddling the Inland Revenue. Bet cursed Alec's dodgy dealings, and finally took off her wedding ring, swearing she was never going to put it on again.

The following year crooked councillor Harry Potts informed Bet that Weatherfield Council was planning to widen Rosamund

◄ The Gilroys' relationship is over when Alec leaves for Southampton. ► Stella informs Bet that the brewery is selling the Rovers.

Street and demolish the Rovers. He promised to drip-feed her vital information and fight her corner. In return and to keep him in favour, she gave him drinks on the house. Worried about her future, she confided in her mate Stella Rigby at the White Swan. To her astonishment, Stella revealed Harry had also been telling her the council were about to demolish the White Swan. They realised they'd been taken for mugs, with Harry conning the pair of them, and so they decided to take their revenge. After confirmation from Rovers' regular councillor Alf Roberts that there were no plans to widen Rosamund Street, she and Stella invited Harry to Reg Holdsworth's engagement party in the Rovers, revealed they knew the truth and then forced him to buy free drinks all round in exchange for their silence!

Bet continued to manage the boozer until a shock announcement in 1995 when Newton & Ridley revealed it was selling six of its pubs as part of the company's restructuring plan, and on that list was the Rovers Return Inn with an asking price of £68,000. She was given first refusal, but a meeting with the bank manager failed to secure her the necessary funds. Despite this bitter blow, she was back behind the bar that same evening with a forced smile and cheery chat for her loyal customers and friends.

'You see this smile, Betty? It's not really a smile. It's the lid on a scream.'

Bet

23

◀ ▶ Bet couldn't wait to tell Raquel she was buying the pub – but flees the street after a fallout with investor Rita.

When her lifelong pal Rita Sullivan showed an interest in investing, Bet perked up no end and, with her hopes raised, she managed to persuade the brewery to drop the price by £2,000. On a high she jumped the gun and started blabbing to the staff that she and Rita were going into partnership and buying the Rovers together. On hearing Bet had already broadcast the news before they'd reached an agreement, Rita decided not to go through with the deal, which led to an almighty row between the two formidable women.

Heartbroken Bet let rip at Rita, accusing her of only having money because she'd married into it. 'Without Len you'd be nowt but a clapped-out chorus girl,' she spat. Meanwhile Rita retorted that Bet had always been jealous of her because she'd married Len. In a painful and raw exchange they fought their way through past hurts, leaving both women acutely aware they'd torn their friendship apart and there was no going back.

Now more desperate than ever and with time running out, Bet swallowed her pride and asked Alec's wealthy granddaughter Vicky for a £66,000 loan. She was left feeling patronised and humiliated when Vicky turned her down, instead offering to buy Bet a small home and charge her a nominal rent. Bet rounded on her, pointing out she'd loved Vicky enough to house her for free.

Broken and humiliated, she threw Vicky out of the pub before turning on the startled customers and also turfing them all into the street. Slamming shut the doors of the pub, Bet packed her bags, put on her finest leopard-skin prints, took one last lingering look at the premises she loved so much and stepped into a taxi bound for pastures new. After a turbulent and eventful few decades on the same street, Bet Lynch had finally had enough and it was time to say ta-ra to the Rovers and Weatherfield.

Here come the Duckies…

Discovering Bet had gone, barmaid Liz McDonald set her sights on the Rovers and put Number 11 on the market for £29,950 to pay for it. Speculation grew as to who would be the first actual owners of Rovers when it was sold at a public auction, but no one could have predicted the new landlords would turn out to be the Duckworths! Former pot-man Jack had used a surprise inheritance from his brother Cliff to change their status and buy the local pub, and gobby Vera swelled with pride as her name was etched over the doorway – Jack's name had to be omitted due to his previous run-ins with the police (a speeding ticket and a fine for parking in a disabled space).

'What does it say when his wife's name is over the door? This man is henpecked, this man is under his wife's thumb, this man is clearly a feckless article!'

Jack sulks as Vera becomes licensee

◄ ► Smiles all round for new owners the Duckworths; but it isn't long before Jack has both Vera and Betty on his back.

Not everyone was quite so thrilled; the McDonalds were gutted to have been pipped at the post and long-serving barmaid Betty tutted that Mrs Walker must be turning in her grave. Regardless of any criticism, Vera took to her new role of landlady with gusto, immediately winding up Betty by insisting that she clean as well as cook – which led to Betty storming out in disgust. Undeterred, Vera trumpeted she could manage without Betty and the hotpot she cooked would be just as good as the veteran barmaid's. It wasn't, and after plenty of grovelling Betty was persuaded to return. Meanwhile butcher Fred Elliott offered Jack a good deal on his pies, but the customers complained about the taste and soon Jack fell ill with a stomach bug. He accused Fred of poisoning them all, but Fred in turn blamed Jack, saying the culprit was the cheap sickly new beer he was serving.

Balancing the books was never the Duckworths' strong point (they only made £4.50 profit on their first day) and their finances went even further down the pan when, much to Vera's dismay, Jack splashed out on a share of a dud racehorse called 'Betty's Hotshot'. In 1997 the couple were landed with a whopping tax bill of £17,600 and to pay it off Jack sold half of the Rovers behind Vera's back. Their new business partner was previous

The Stats

Pints
1,440 pints pulled per week
3.5 million pints served *

Crisps
48 bags sold per week
2,500 per year
120,000 bags sold *

Hotpot
84 dished up per week
4,300 per year
200,000 sold

since records began in 1961

tenant Alec Gilroy, who had returned to Weatherfield and had his beady little eye on his old stomping ground once again.

When an incensed Vera discovered what Jack had done she walloped him, accused him of selling out on their dreams and locked him out of the pub. A shamefaced Jack spent the night sleeping in the yard with his pigeons but was stirred into action when Alec told him to fight back and get back to the pub. Vera was one step ahead of them and had changed the locks, so the pair tricked their way back in by posing as draymen. Once inside, Jack managed to calm Vera down by promising he wouldn't let Alec rule the roost.

It was soon obvious that their arrangement was never going to work as they continued to rub each other up the wrong way, so in 1998 the Duckworths cut their losses and sold out to Alec. On hearing his plans to evict them from their home as well, Jack and Vera barricaded themselves in their bedroom. While Alec turned the heating off in an attempt to freeze them out, their supportive neighbours delivered hot meals by climbing up a ladder outside. Eventually Alec admitted defeat and by the time the Duckworths ended their siege, former barmaid Natalie Barnes had taken the reins as licensee.

► Natalie only has eyes for two-timing Ian Bentley.
▼ The Duckies are unimpressed by Natalie's back-room makeover.

Natalie takes the reins...

With her name now over the door Natalie set about making some changes. Her first task was to restructure the staff and while Jack was happy to return to his old job as cellar-man, Vera was aghast at having to take orders from her former employee.

Natalie's time in Weatherfield wasn't the happiest. She'd bought the pub to take her mind off her recently murdered husband, Des Barnes, who had been killed trying to protect her son Tony while he was being attacked by a gang of drug dealers to whom he owed a lot of money. Buying the Rovers didn't make life any better for Natalie, though. Having gained a reputation as a home-wrecker thanks to her affair with married man Kevin Webster, she hoped she'd found true love with sales rep Ian Bentley. Unfortunately for Natalie he turned out to be engaged to Rita's former foster daughter, Sharon Gaskell. When the affair came to light a livid Rita laid into Natalie, calling her a hard-faced bitch.

Worse was yet to come when the body of her estranged son Tony was discovered by her builder boyfriend, Vinny, on a site in Victoria Street. The police told her Tony had been

'By hell, lady, I've met some hard-faced bitches in my time but you take the bloody gold medal!'

Rita to Natalie

beaten over the head with a baseball bat and they'd only been able to identify him by his dental records. Distraught and horrified by his grisly death, Natalie hit the bottle, but she was confused as to why she was grieving so much when she'd always held Tony responsible for Des's untimely demise. When she was drunk, she laid into the bewildered regulars, calling them two-faced hypocrites.

Then there was the double whammy of finding out that not only was she pregnant, but that Vinny was sleeping with her sister Debs behind her back. Fed up of the bad memories that surrounded her in Weatherfield, she decided to start a new life in the Cotswolds.

▲ Landlady Natalie shows Leanne the ropes.
◀ Natalie is devastated by her son Tony's death.
▶ Fred, Duggie and Mike bag the boozer.

The Rovers is saved...

'You may be an expert running your eye over the hindquarters of a cow for a nice piece of rump steak, but we're going to need a more subtle approach if we're gonna find ourselves a decent bar manager.'

Mike to Fred

When the residents discovered Natalie intended to sell the pub to the Boozy chain, a company who wanted to rebrand the Rovers as the Boozy Newt and aim it a younger, trendier clientele, there was uproar. This was when local businessman Duggie Ferguson, factory owner Mike Baldwin and foghorn-voiced butcher Fred Elliott came together and hatched a plan to save the Rovers from its Boozy fate by collectively buying it. The trio drew straws to see who should be licensee and Duggie was the lucky winner.

However, when it came to running the Rovers, the three were a nightmare and constantly interfered with each other's decisions, so much so that the staff didn't know if they were coming or going. The final straw was a meagre pay offer and the introduction of tarty new uniforms. 'You know, skimpy, with lots of leg and boob showing,' explained angry barmaid Geena Gregory.

Having had enough of their poor management style, bar staff Geena, Betty and Toyah Battersby went on strike and stood outside the pub with banners saying 'We Are Not Slaves!' and 'Boycott the Rovers!' When Fred attempted to rip down their handiwork, Toyah stood firm: 'We won't stand for this bully-boy management,' she snarled. When he called her a silly little girl she snapped back that he was a sexist pig, which seemed to cut Fred to the core. 'A pig is a very noble animal!' he spluttered, affronted. Meanwhile the women of Weatherfield were on the barmaids' side. 'Good on ya,' smirked Janice. 'It'll teach those dirty old men a lesson.' A determined Mike stood outside trying to drum up business, but no one would cross the picket line and in the end he gave in to their demands.

Duggie became increasingly fed up with Mike and Fred, whose interest in the pub had started to wane, and told them he wanted to dissolve the partnership,

'You're a has-been, Duggie. And this is a backstreet pub. So less of the big I am!'
Peter on being sacked

◄ Duggie's strict regime doesn't go down well with the bar staff.
▲ Shelley and Geena sulk when Eve becomes their new boss.

persuading them to sell out to an anonymous buyer at a knock-down rate. Once the deal was done he revealed he was actually the mystery buyer. Mike and Fred were furious, with the butcher announcing he was boycotting the premises. Duggie had other matters to worry about, though, when two reps from the Weights and Measures Department of Weatherfield Council Trading Standards suddenly appeared to carry out tests on the whisky after a tip-off that it had been watered down. Duggie suspected Toyah of being the grass and sacked her, but it turned out it was boozing barman Peter Barlow who'd been watering down the spirits to cover his tracks and Mike was the snitch – he'd done it to get his own back for Duggie's unscrupulous con.

Later that year Duggie had set his sights on bigger things and sold up in order to buy the Weatherfield Rugby League Social Club. When he announced his move, barmaid Geena and her shopkeeper boyfriend Dev Alahan expressed an interest in buying, as did fellow barmaid Shelley Unwin and her boyfriend Peter, and butcher Fred and his new wife Eve Elliott, née Sykes. Duggie decided auctioning off the pub would be the fairest way, with Fred winning out with a last-minute bid of £76,000.

Fred takes centre stage...

The newlyweds moved in their belongings the next day and Fred arranged for a sign painter to put Eve's name up over the Rovers' door as landlady. To his horror and Eve's fury, the sign painter put Betty's name over the door by accident. He eventually managed to rectify the situation and the pair settled into life as publicans. But cracks soon started to appear in their relationship and three months later a heartbroken Fred discovered Eve was a bigamist and threw her out. Although unlucky in love, Fred never stopped hoping he'd find his very own happy-ever-after and proposed to, amongst others, hairdresser Audrey Roberts (who turned him down) and Thai bride Orchid, who was later exposed as a money-chasing con-artist.

'He's a man of a certain age. Put a gorilla in a short skirt and a blonde wig, and he'd be cooing sweet nothings at it.'

Bev on Fred

Feeling overworked and underpaid due to the staffing issues, Geena and Shelley both had their eyes on becoming relief manager. But Fred had other ideas and approached Bet Lynch to make a return. When she declined his offer, he turned to his rather snotty acquaintance Lillian Spencer, who arrived with her bird 'Dynah the Mynah' in tow. Lillian made it quite clear she found the Rovers a comedown from the grandeur of her previous establishments. She sniffed: 'When I ran the Xanadu bar at the Majestic Hotel, Cleethorpes, aah, that was the high water mark of my career. Suffice to say that since those halcyon days the tide has gone out rather further than I had hoped.'

Both Shelley and Geena took an instant dislike to Lillian and there was an outcry when she barred Norris for being rude about the state of the place. Rita then gave her a piece of her mind for barring Norris and for being ill-mannered to barmaid Shelley – so Lillian banned a stunned Rita as well!

Fred was worried by Lillian's trigger-happy approach to barring his regulars but had even more reason for concern when her son Tim turned up at the pub, followed by her daughter Danielle. The unwelcome Lillian and her family were taking over the place and Fred fretted about the best way to get rid of her. Adding to his troubles, Shelley and Geena informed him if Lillian stayed, they were leaving. Fortunately for Fred he was saved from the nasty job of sacking her when Lillian suddenly received a call from a friend offering her a better position in Marple and the family vacated the pub, much to everyone's relief.

Pleased with the way Shelley had coped with running the Rovers while Fred was on holiday he decided to keep her on full-time as manageress. Shelley was a bubbly and bright barmaid who stood for no nonsense, except when it came to relationships and romance. She believed her marriage to Peter Barlow to be a happy one but when a woman called Lucy arrived with a wedding album showing her own wedding to Peter, she realised the Barlow rat was a bigamist. Not only was he married to another woman, Shelley was gobsmacked to learn that Lucy and Peter even had a baby boy together called Simon. Realising her own wedding to Peter had been a sham as he'd married Lucy first, Shelley threw Peter out and was left utterly dejected and destroyed. He tried to talk to her but Shelley shrieked at him that he was barred from the pub and from her life.

After her ordeal at the hands of two-timing Peter, Shelley probably thought men couldn't get any worse, but then she met local builder Charlie Stubbs. Initially she was taken in by his rugged smile and flattering flirtation, but these charms soon made way for a much more sinister side after she'd fallen for him hook, line and sinker.

Thanks to his bullying, Shelley became a shadow of her former strong-minded self. The manipulative, cold-hearted control freak gradually chipped away at her self-confidence and self-worth,

'The usual please, chuck!'

While the regulars have always stuck to their favourite tipples – Rita and her vodka tonic, Roy and his tomato juice, Mike Baldwin and his large scotch – for free-spirited eccentric, Mary Taylor, it seems variety is the spice of life. Her quirky drinks orders have included gin & apple juice, peach schnapps & slimline, Guinness & blackcurrant and a thirst-quenching Dubonnet & bitter lemon.

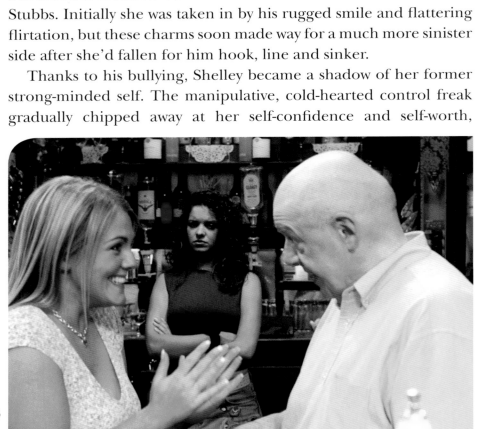

Shelley is delighted when Fred makes her permanent manager.
▲ Charlie begins destroy Shelley's self-confidence.

twisting her behaviour at every turn, criticising her weight and her looks and ripping apart her personality. Charlie isolated Shelley from everyone around her and chased every bit of skirt he could behind her back, including Liz McDonald. Shelley sacked Liz when she told her what had happened, choosing to believe her lying, cheating boyfriend instead.

Charlie even put up a poster behind the bar saying Shelley was losing weight for charity and that he'd give £5 for every pound she lost. An increasingly insecure Shelley felt humiliated and resorted to plastic surgery to make herself perfect for her boyfriend. He forbade her friendship with Sunita Alahan and, following his cruellest instruction of all, she even disowned her own mother Bev.

By the end of their relationship she was a gibbering wreck, often seen cowering in the bedroom, too panicked to show her face in the bar. When she eventually saw sense and jilted Charlie at the altar in 2005, it was clear Shelley was finally regaining her confidence and had seen him for the bully he really was.

Free at last to her make her own decisions, Shelley was reunited with her highly-strung mother Bev, who soon had wedding plans of her own and made plans to tie the knot with pub boss Fred. But Bev's relationship with Fred led to tensions behind the bar when Bev started lording it over manageress Shelley, acting like she already owned the place.

Meanwhile, Shelley was feeling stuck in a rut and despondent after a series of disastrous dates, including one with Simon the bus driver who bored her rigid by talking her through his favourite bus routes. In desperation Shelley contacted the brewery and when she was offered a manager's job away from Weatherfield in the Peak District, she jumped at the chance. Bev was gutted and felt she was to blame for pushing her daughter out, but Shelley assured her she was only going because she needed a fresh start.

Just before Shelley left, Charlie found out she was pregnant with his child, and when she refused to have an abortion, he threatened her by pinning her up against the wall in the Rovers' yard. He was stunned when he realised she was no longer scared of him and he'd lost his power. Shelley was back to her old self and was moving on.

Soon wedding preparations between Bev and Fred were in full swing, but on the morning of the ceremony Fred went to visit old flame Audrey Roberts, who had just revealed she regretted turning down his previous offer of marriage. Letting Audrey down gently, he told her he truly loved Bev and intended to marry her. As he was about to leave, he suddenly collapsed and suffered a fatal stroke in Audrey's hallway.

▼ Charlie goes for Shelley in the backyard – but she's no longer scared of him.
▶ Proud owners Steve and Liz toast their new family business.

All smiles for the McDonalds...

Before he passed away, Fred had told Bev he had rented them a cottage near Shelley's pub in the Peak District and suggested, once they were man and wife, they should retire there. Much to the surprise of everyone he had put the Rovers up for sale and had eventually agreed to sell to Liz, who had taken over from Shelley as manageress. But Fred died before the deal was done, and with only a verbal agreement Liz feared the worst. However, after Bev left Weatherfield to live with Shelley, Fred's son Ashley Peacock honoured his father's word and Liz purchased the boozer with the financial backing of her son, Steve.

After so many years of longing Liz had finally got her hands on the pub she'd always wanted, and with her name now officially over the door the former barmaid held a lock-in to celebrate her new status. However, when Steve arrived back from holiday and walked into the

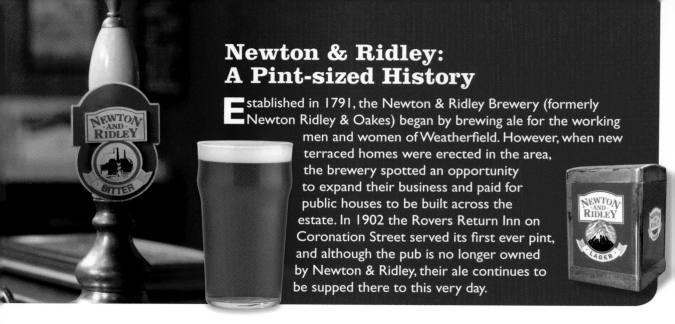

Newton & Ridley:
A Pint-sized History

Established in 1791, the Newton & Ridley Brewery (formerly Newton Ridley & Oakes) began by brewing ale for the working men and women of Weatherfield. However, when new terraced homes were erected in the area, the brewery spotted an opportunity to expand their business and paid for public houses to be built across the estate. In 1902 the Rovers Return Inn on Coronation Street served its first ever pint, and although the pub is no longer owned by Newton & Ridley, their ale continues to be supped there to this very day.

Rovers as the new owner for the first time, he was unimpressed by the state of the place and his mum's cavalier attitude.

In 2007 Liz married idle musician and sometime pot-man Vernon Tomlin, who had forgiven her earlier affair with married drayman Derek. She tied the knot with Vernon despite the fact she still had feelings for her jealous ex Jim – who thumped Vernon and gave him a black eye on their wedding day. She even kept the surname McDonald, her excuse being that that was how she was known in the trade. But the following year she admitted to Vernon she should never have married him. Vernon was devastated and begged her to

◄ Liz cheats on Vernon with silver-fox drayman Derek
▲ Vernon begs Liz to give their marriage a second chance.
▼ Liz is unimpressed when Steve falls for barmaid Michelle.

reconsider but Liz's mind was made up. She later had a fling with younger cab driver Lloyd Mullaney, much to the horror of her son and Lloyd's best mate, Steve.

However, Liz didn't approve of her son's love-matches either. First of all she took against singer-turned-barmaid Michelle Connor, then things got even worse for Liz when Steve broke the news that his rough and ready new girlfriend Becky Granger was moving into

the Rovers because they were engaged. Liz was not impressed and suggested Steve should get a revolving door fitted as he'd only just finished with Michelle.

Liz's relationship with daughter-in-law Becky was often volatile, but occasionally they realised they sort of respected each other. Their feud came to a head in 2011 when Liz laid into Becky after discovering Steve had remortgaged the pub to 'buy' her sister Kylie's son Max. A drunken Becky threw interfering Liz out of the Rovers, telling Liz exactly what she thought of her and pointed out that she was the owner's wife, not Liz.

Deciding it was time to wash her hands of Steve and Becky, Liz collected the last of her things and found herself alone and lonely, drowning her sorrows in a hotel bar – but she was horrified when a businessman mistook her for a prostitute. So when ex-husband and love of her life Jim tracked her down she was overjoyed, although a little cautious, and it was clear they still had feelings for each other.

Steve: *'Whatever gripes you have with each other, you don't bring them to work.'*
Liz: *'Gripes are when staff are late or skive down the cellar. Not when someone bankrupts a pub to buy a kid…'*
Steve attempts to mediate between Liz and Becky

◀ Steve and Kylie watch on as Liz and Becky lock horns.
▶ Exes Liz and Jim are briefly reunited.

They agreed to give their complicated relationship another chance and she made up with Steve and Becky. Together Jim and Liz planned to buy the Rovers back from Steve, but unable to bring himself to disappoint Liz by telling her he'd failed to raise the necessary funds, Jim resorted to robbery.

The first Liz and Steve knew of it was when a police escort arrived at the Rovers to collect them to speak to him and they were horrified to find an armed Jim holding hostages in a building society. Jim tried to call Liz on her mobile but the police blocked the call. An angry Steve confronted the negotiator – Liz was the only person who could calm his dad down, which she did, and after evacuating the hostages he was arrested, leaving Liz ashamed and heartbroken.

The next day she visited him in prison and apologised for the pressure she'd put on him to buy the Rovers. It was only a pub after all and their relationship was worth more than bricks and mortar. She agreed to wait for him but grew increasingly downbeat as the burden of her commitment dawned on her. That night, after reminiscing about her time in the Rovers with Steve and Becky, Liz tearfully locked up and, without telling a soul, fled for a new life in Spain. But Liz couldn't stay away from Weatherfield for ever, and two years later she was back behind the bar where she belonged.

'You think you're the queen of the Rovers? You're a tart with a bus pass!'

Becky to Liz

With Liz out of the picture Steve needed a new manager, and after she impressed him during her interview, he gave the job to experienced bar hand Stella Price – although he wasn't quite so chuffed when Stella unexpectedly moved her partner Karl Munro and her daughter Eva into the Rovers as well. Giving the place the once over, Karl told Stella he wasn't impressed with what he saw

and couldn't understand why she'd wanted to leave their previous pub – but the reason for Stella's choice of the Coronation Street boozer soon became clear.

She'd only been at the helm for a matter of weeks before it was revealed Stella was Leanne Barlow's real mother. She'd abandoned her as a baby and was desperate to make amends. On her arrival on the street she'd quickly befriended Leanne, who had no idea the new pub landlady was in fact her birth mother. Stella helped organise a surprise party for Leanne's 30th in the Rovers, and became emotional when Peter made a heartfelt speech saying how much he loved Leanne.

In the back room she explained to a shocked Eva that Leanne was actually her daughter, but Leanne overheard and stormed out through the bar as the regulars started singing 'Happy Birthday'. Eva was furious to discover she'd got a sister she knew nothing about

▲ ▼ Steve interviews Stella – she takes the manager's job to be near secret daughter Leanne.
▶ Stella pulls rank on Karl when he installs a television in the bar.

and snapped at Stella that she may have gained a new daughter but she'd lost her old one. In the heat of the moment Stella slapped her but immediately regretted it.

Stella tried to explain her desertion to Leanne, insisting she couldn't cope back then as she was so young herself and living with Leanne's dad had proved very difficult – especially whilst trying to manage with a new baby – so she had walked out. She'd later returned and tried to get her daughter back but Les's mum had refused to let her anywhere near her. Initially Leanne snapped that she wanted nothing to do with her, but she began to mellow when she saw how sincere Stella was, and soon mother and daughter were determined to make up for all those lost years.

Stella settled into life at the pub but her layabout not-so-better-half Karl proved to be more of a hindrance than a help. One afternoon, after popping into town for some retail therapy with Leanne, she returned to find Karl had installed a huge flat-screen TV in the Rovers. Most of the regulars walked out due to the noise and when Ken confronted Karl about the new satellite dish causing problems with the TV reception at Number 1, he just shrugged his shoulders and refused to budge. Stella thumped him in frustration and when Karl finally removed the satellite dish she left him stranded on the roof of the Rovers to get her own back.

But Karl decided on another approach and within days he stole Jason's van, torched it, and anonymously gave Jason's description in the hope that the police would think it was an insurance scam. Despite knowing Karl was behind it, Jason held back from using his fists and informed Karl his plan had only brought him and Stella closer together and he was moving into the pub. When Karl tampered with the Rovers' plumbing, which led to an overnight power failure and water leak, he knew his rival would get the blame again, but once more his plotting backfired when the Rovers' candle-lit evening with a war-time-style sing-along led by Rita was a resounding success.

Karl was further annoyed when he heard Jason had decided to knock his building career on the head and accept Stella's offer of a job behind the bar. 'I wonder how long it'll be until he's got his name over the door,' mused Stella's mum Gloria Price, much to Karl's fury. 'Somehow it all comes good for him,' he muttered to Tommy Duckworth at the bar. 'He's got all the luck – my girlfriend, my pub, my whole flamin' life.'

Becoming more menacing and unpredictable by the minute, Karl stepped up his win-back-Stella campaign, but no one could've predicted his next devastating move (see page 180) which would change the face of the Rovers Return forever...

> '*Folk want cold beer and hotpot, not warm ale and scratchings by candlelight.*'
> **Stella on the power cut**

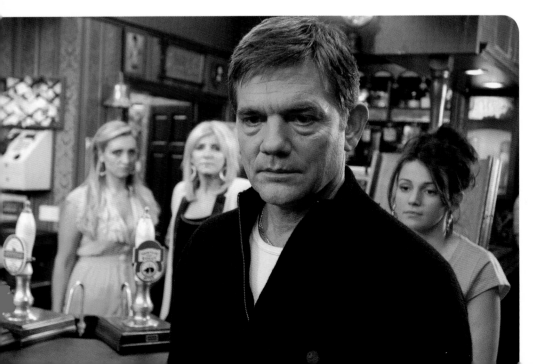

◄ Karl takes matters into his own hands to win Stella back.

THE GREAT PUB OF THE YEAR SCAM

It was only for a quiet life that Stella finally gave in and agreed that her mum Gloria could enter the Rovers into *Lancashire Leisure* magazine's Pub of the Year competition. What she didn't know was that Gloria had entered it as a B&B, so when Stella arrived home early from a hen weekend, she was somewhat taken aback to find her mum fussing over a complete stranger in the back room and was forced to play along by pretending to be another paying guest.

As Gloria had predicted, the satisfied visitor had been one of the judges, but her joy at winning the competition was short-lived when Mr Mathers, editor of *Lancashire Leisure* magazine, arrived to present the award and read out some of the glowing customer feedback on the pub. There was an outcry from the regulars who insisted they hadn't written the comments and it soon became apparent Gloria had penned the praise herself.

One such that was supposedly from Norris Cole read: 'At the end of a long and weary day, when the old feet are aching and the pace of modern life is getting on top of me, the only place I want to be is the Rovers Return, Weatherfield, where a kind word from Gloria and a leisurely half resets my compass, making the world feel familiar once again.' Norris was outraged. 'I wrote that she was vulgar and I wrote it anonymously!' he shrieked.

The Rovers was disqualified, and in front of the *Gazette* reporter a tussle broke out as an unrepentant Gloria desperately tried to grab the winner's plaque from Mr Mathers!

'I've only ever won one thing in my life. Butlins, 1959. Miss Chubby, Charming and Cheerful Competition. Not exactly something you want to put on your mantelpiece, is it? But this…'

Gloria fantasises about winning

Running the Rovers

1937
Just before the outbreak of World War II, publican Jack Walker takes over the pub with his new bride Annie.

1961
Ambitious relief manager Vince Plummer covers while the Walkers are on holiday – he slates the pub for being old fashioned.

1961
Annie draws up plans to knock the three bars into one – the idea is dropped when the regulars disapprove.

1963
Annie is reported to the brewery for selling non-regulation Cyprus sherry over the counter.

1992
Alec leaves for Southampton and sells the licence back to the brewery. Bet ends their marriage in order to stay on as manager.

1987
Bet buys the licence from the brewery with £15,000 borrowed from Alec Gilroy – they marry and run the pub together.

1986
The pub is destroyed by fire (see page 174). Bet oversees the refurbishments and the three bars are knocked into one.

1985
Barmaid Bet becomes the brewery's first unmarried manager of the Rovers Return.

1984
Billy returns to take over the licence but he alienates customers and ends up selling the tenancy back to the brewery.

1984
Pot-man Fred becomes temporary manager when Annie retires. But he's struck down with pneumonia and Frank Harvey replaces him.

1993
Barmaid Liz McDonald acts as relief manager when Bet holidays in Tenerife with Rita Sullivan.

1995
Rodney Bostock holds the fort when Bet quits after failing to find the funds to buy the pub from the brewery.

1995
Due to an unexpected windfall Jack and Vera Duckworth are the surprise new owners of the Rovers Return.

1997
Cash-flow problems prompt Jack to sell 50 per cent of the pub to Alec Gilroy, much to Vera's fury.

1998
Jack and Vera are forced to sell their remaining share to Alec, who becomes their boss while they continue to live and work in the pub.

2013
The Rovers is refurbished after a fire ravages the pub (see page 180) and the McDonalds return to the helm.

2012
Following his affair with barmaid Sunita Alahan, Karl moves out and gives Stella his half of the pub, making her the sole owner.

2012
Stella and her partner Karl Munro jump at the chance to buy the premises from Steve.

2011
Following Liz's flit to Spain, Steve takes on newcomer Stella Price as pub manager.

1965
When she is elected chairperson of the Lady Victuallers, Annie's opening speech is nine pages long!

1966
On returning from holiday in Ireland Annie is horrified to find a snooker match in progress, organised by relief manager Brenda Riley.

1968
Annie is furious when the demolition of the Mission and Ellison's raincoat factory leaves her newly painted pub covered in dust.

1970
After Jack's sudden death in July, Annie becomes the sole licensee.

1973
Billy Walker's spell as manager ends when he slips away, leaving gambling debts.

1973
The regulars complain when relief manager Glyn Thomas introduces a one-armed bandit and an organist. However, his introduction of hot food is a hit.

1981
Gordon Lewis runs the pub while Annie is on a cruise. His strict regime prompts a staff walkout.

1980
Annie extends the food menu and enjoys ringing the bell when the food is ready – once for Betty Turpin, twice for Bet and three times for Fred Gee.

1978
Albert Tatlock accuses Annie of starting a food-poisoning epidemic when everyone becomes ill after eating her pies.

1977
Annie returns from visiting her daughter Joan to find the draymen on strike, so she is forced to ration the remaining beer in her cellar.

1999
When Alec sells the pub to barmaid Natalie Barnes, Jack and Vera lose their home.

2000
To stop the proposed sale to the Boozy Newt chain, regulars Mike Baldwin, Fred Elliott and Duggie Ferguson join forces to buy the premises.

2001
Duggie becomes sole owner and is nominated for landlord of the year. But he's rude to an undercover judge and comes 271st, much to Betty's amusement.

2001
Fred buys the pub at auction, installing new wife Eve as landlady. She turns out to be a bigamist and Fred becomes licensee.

2002
Super-snob Lillian Spencer is recruited by Fred as manager, but after antagonising the regulars, she moves to pastures new.

2011
Lloyd Mullaney stands in as manager when Steve and Becky join Liz on holiday.

2008
Liz employs Poppy Morales as bar manager – but she's sacked after a few months for upsetting Betty.

2007
After she's caught lighting up in the Ladies, Liz enjoys christening the newly erected smoking shelter in the backyard.

2006
After Fred's death Steve McDonald buys the Rovers and his mum Liz finally becomes licensee.

2004
Dissatisfied with Shelley's work, Fred offers the job to her mum Bev. The atmosphere is strained until Shelley is reinstated.

2002
No-nonsense barmaid Shelley Unwin becomes the pub's permanent manager.

Fun and Games

From the Weatherfield Olympics in 1984, where Betty proved herself to be the unexpected queen of wellie-wangling, via beer-swigging challenges and cross-dressing bowls matches, to Steve McDonald's failure to demonstrate any ball control during a five-a-side defeat against the Flying Horse in 2012, there's nothing like a spot of inter-pub rivalry to keep the Rovers regulars bonded together...

Wacky Races!

1978

Eddie Yeats entered the Rovers in a charity pram-race pub-crawl against the Flying Horse. Dressed as babies the men had to drink a pint in each pub while the women pushed the prams. The race included four pubs and they had to go to each pub twice. But a breathless Mavis Riley nearly did herself an injury lugging Eddie around, the pram couldn't cope either and its wheels buckled. First to finish were Suzie Birchall and Steve Fisher, but they were disqualified when steward Ena Sharples revealed Suzie had swigged Steve's last pint.

Fred: *'I'll not look like a baby – I'll look like Old Mother Riley in this!'*

Gail: *'You will when you've got your bonnet on and your dummy stuck in your mouth!'*

Fred's unimpressed with his costume

Question Time

1992

In a bid to increase profits, Newton & Ridley ordered Bet to enter an inter-pub quiz, but a practice night ended in chaos thanks to lecherous quizmaster Reg Holdsworth who was more interested in winning Bet's affections than following the rules of the game. Ditzy barmaid Raquel Wolstenhulme acted as his glamorous assistant, but a stand-up row erupted between the teams when Mavis, Vera, Gail and Deirdre insisted the opposition – Jack, Curly, Martin and Derek – were trying to diddle them out of a point. Watching the commotion was disapproving brewery boss Richard Willmore, who told a downbeat Bet he'd give her another couple of months to boost trade or she'd be fired.

2001

Despite quizmaster Duggie Ferguson being unable to get the hang of his crackling radio mic, the Rovers' quiz night was a resounding success and Norris, Curly and Rita's team bagged the £50 prize money by one point. But the most entertaining part of the evening was when Sunita Parekh, who'd been dating Duggie, dumped him in the back room saying he was too old for her. But Duggie was still wearing his radio mic and the whole pub listened in through the PA system as he begged her to reconsider – and for the first time all night everyone could hear him loud and clear!

2000

Barmaid Geena organised a Mr & Mrs Competition that saw the Peacocks row over their answers – Maxine was furious when Ashley suggested she snored and picked her nose. Roy and Hayley Cropper were declared the winners, but ignorant Les Battersby tried to overrule the result, declaring the couple were actually Mr & Mr.

2007

Self-titled 'Quiz-meister' Vernon Tomlin rapidly got on Liz's wick by crashing a cymbal every time he took to the mic during the Rovers' pub quiz. His moment in the spotlight was then interrupted by a fight in the street between Peter Barlow and Charlie Stubbs. While his opponents piled outside to break-up the brawl, Norris sneaked a peek at Roy's team's answers to give himself a one point win.

Michelle: *'Is he going to make a habit of hitting that cymbal?'*
Liz: *'Not if he wants to live.'*
On quiz-meister Vernon

> *'If the water starts rising, get the aerial up and hang your knickers off. It won't call any lifeguards but at least it'll keep the sharks off.'*
>
> **Fred**

> *'"Come for a little trip", he says, "in the Rover", he says. We end up shipwrecked, marooned and covered in cow-muck!'*
>
> **Bet**

Car Trouble
1983

To ensure Fred's hands stayed on the steering wheel and didn't wander anywhere else, Bet invited Betty along when the pot-man asked her out in his Rover for a bank-holiday picnic. Needless to say, Fred was irked that Betty's presence had thwarted his romantic intentions, but the day took an even worse turn when the car propelled itself into the middle of a lake with the two startled barmaids still in it. Bet reached for the brake, but it came off in her hand and the car began to sink. Seething, she ordered Fred to give them a piggyback to dry land – but he ruined his knight-in-shining-armour moment by plonking her down onto a cow pat!

Pub Poetry

1993

Bet was bemused to find herself promoting a brewery poetry competition but Mavis and Derek Wilton were thrilled, eager to put pen to paper. Pompous as ever, Derek criticised Mavis's offering, 'Our Friend the Fox', but couldn't wait to give her a sneak preview of his own attempt while they waited for the competition to begin.

'Mavis, my Marilyn...' he began. 'She was a legend of her time, nations applauded, whole continents were in her thrall. The world resounded with the name Monroe. But there was another goddess, of flesh, not celluloid. In Weatherfield, not Hollywood. One who, for me, outmatched, outshone, and yes, outlived Monroe. Who needs the silver screen when I have the silver in her hair? Who needs the wind-blown skirt when I can nightly gaze upon the lifting hem of my own personal Monroe? Her breasts are downy like the peach...'

Mavis's mouth fell open, 'I beg your pardon?' she gasped. 'It's adult company and it's 1993,' Derek scolded. 'I can say breasts.' But Mavis was outraged. 'Yes, but you're talking about me and peaches are hairy,' she wailed. 'If you read that out loud, I shall shout, I shall heckle, I shall throw something!' Adding with a hiss: 'Pornographer!'

The Wiltons withdrew from the competition, leaving the only other entrant, gravel-voiced pensioner Phyllis Pearce, as the winner.

Much to the embarrassment of purse-lipped Percy Sugden, her 'Ode to Percy' brought the house down. 'When God made Percy he was smiling. He took two lusty arms and took two sturdy legs and he stuck them on the body of my darling. And if he wants to buy me flowers he can do it any day. And if he wants to misbehave with me, I won't stand in his way!'

> *'When God made Percy he was smiling. He took two lusty arms and took two sturdy legs and he stuck them on the body of my darling.'*
>
> **Phyllis**

THIS SATURDAY
CORONATION STREET OLYMPICS
ROVERS RETURN v FLYING HORSE

Going for Gold!
1984

Everyone rallied round when Billy Walker suggested a Coronation Street Olympics against the Flying Horse to raise funds for Emily's church appeal. Brian and Gail Tilsley won the three-legged race, but when Bet tried to win her egg and spoon race, she cheated and glued an egg to a spoon with her gum. She was rumbled and came last when she was forced to use a normal egg and spoon. Vera Duckworth finished first but was disqualified for knocking the egg off the spoon of the woman in front of her, leaving a delighted Hilda Ogden as the winner. Betty Turpin was victorious in the welly-throwing contest, and when the male regulars won a tug of war the Rovers Return athletes were crowned champions.

Sid: *'How d'you get muscles like that?'*

Betty: *'Practice. Chuckin' folk out the Rovers.'*

Betty's welly-throwing impresses the Flying Horse's Sid Duffy

The Beautiful Game

1969

The Rovers took on the Flying Horse with a footie team consisting of Len, Cyril, Dickie, Audrey, Stan and Hilda, with Betty as captain and Albert as head coach. Tactics to win included kidnapping the Flying Horse's mascot, a donkey called Dolores. When Dolores refused to budge (and stamped on Stan's toe), Albert and Hilda attempted to get the Flying Horse's star player Tommy Deakin too drunk to play, but they just ended up legless themselves. At half-time the score was 3–2 to the Flying Horse, but after Hilda scored a surprise equaliser the Rovers were declared the winners on the toss of a coin.

Witches' Brew

2003

The locals attempted to out-spook each other at the first-ever Rovers' Halloween night. Shelley, Janice and Eileen ended up as a coven of witches, Tyrone was a pasty-faced zombie, Nick was Dracula and Fred was an uncanny Frankenstein's monster with a bolt through his neck. Steve was horrified to discover his werewolf facial hair had come from the salon's floor – and he was wearing Rita, Les and Vera's off-cuts!

'I thought, what's the most frightening thing I can come as? They had no Les Battersby outfits so I had to go wi' next best thing.'

Janice dressed as a witch

1996 Having felt the presence of long-departed Ivy Brennan on the landing of Number 5, Vera was convinced her best friend's ghost had followed her to the Rovers. Hubby Jack persuaded Vera to talk to the local paper in the hope that it would pull in more trade and he even bought t-shirts bearing the legend: 'The Rovers Return – try our spirits' emblazoned on the front, and 'Our beers are out of this world too' on the back. Jesting about wet t-shirt competitions, Jack made barmaid Raquel try one on for size, but Vera was not amused at Jack using Ivy to make money. 'Here's a wet t-shirt,' she barked and poured a pint of ale over him.

'You've heard of the Bride of Frankenstein? Well I'm the Husband of Vera Duckworth.'

Jack on his lack of costume

1993 When the fortune-teller Bet had booked cancelled at the last moment, Maureen Naylor volunteered her mother to step in. With a scarf wrapped around her head, Mystic Maud Grimes successfully read palms for Vera, Curly and Bet – mainly due to the fact that Maureen was in the background frantically miming clues to her about them!

Rovers' Ravers

2004

Coached by Jack Duckworth, the ladies amateur bowling team 'The Rovers' Ravers' made it to the final of the pub league, only to find themselves one player down when Hayley was disqualified after Edie Bagshawe, the tough-as-nails coach of the Slaughtermans Arms' squad, discovered she'd once played as a semi-professional for East Lancashire under the name of Harold.

Donning a blonde wig to become 'Ida Fagg', it was up to Jack to save the day. With his shaved legs, lip-gloss and fake boobs he made a surprisingly convincing woman, so much so Vera became convinced that Jack and Ida were having an affair. 'She looks like the kind of old trollop that our Jack would knock around with,' she scowled as she watched the match.

With the scores level the deciding bowl was between Jack and Edie and it was at that moment that Jack's cover was blown. But Jack had an ace up his sleeve: he'd recognised Edie too – as Eddie Bagshawe. With Edie's secret also out of the bag, the pair agreed to keep quiet and let the best woman win, with 'Ida' clinching the trophy for the Ravers.

> **'She looks like the kind of old trollop that our Jack would knock around with.'**
>
> **Vera on Ida**

Bullseye!

2006

Factory boss Paul Connor set up a darts challenge between the machinists and a management team of Paul, Liam, Danny and Michelle to decide the scale of their Christmas do. It all hinged on his final throw but the dart fell out onto the floor; when Janice took her turn she won the contest for the jubilant workers. Determined not to lose face, Paul insisted he'd lost the match on purpose to boost staff morale – but no one believed him!

Dressing Down

1993

Unable to pay his rent at the Duckworths', down-on-his-luck Doug Murray was forced to spend the night in a rusty old camper van, whilst Jack refused to return his clothes until he coughed up. Bet was furious when he appeared in the Rovers in nothing but his boxers and instructed Jack to dress him immediately!

71

Our Day Out
1967

Darryl the Runaway Rat
2012

With their landlord, Steve McDonald, determined to sell Number 13, tenants Tracy McDonald and Beth Tinker did everything they could to put off potential purchasers – even allowing teenager Craig's pet rat Darryl to run amok. Later, in the Rovers, his mum Beth reached into her handbag for her furry mobile phone cover – but it was furry Darryl she pulled to her ear! Behind the bar, rat-phobic barmaid Eva Price dropped the pint glass she was holding and screamed the house down as Darryl scampered away. It was eagle-eyed barmaid Sunita Alahan who spotted him scuttling across the bar just as the health inspector arrived for his scheduled visit. She managed to hide the squirming rodent in her clenched fist and, much to everyone's relief, the pub passed the inspection with flying colours.

'If only every pub had your impeccable standards. Strictly entre nous, you knock spots off the Flying Horse. You should see the state of their panini maker. It's almost Dickensian...'

Health inspector Mr Brownlow

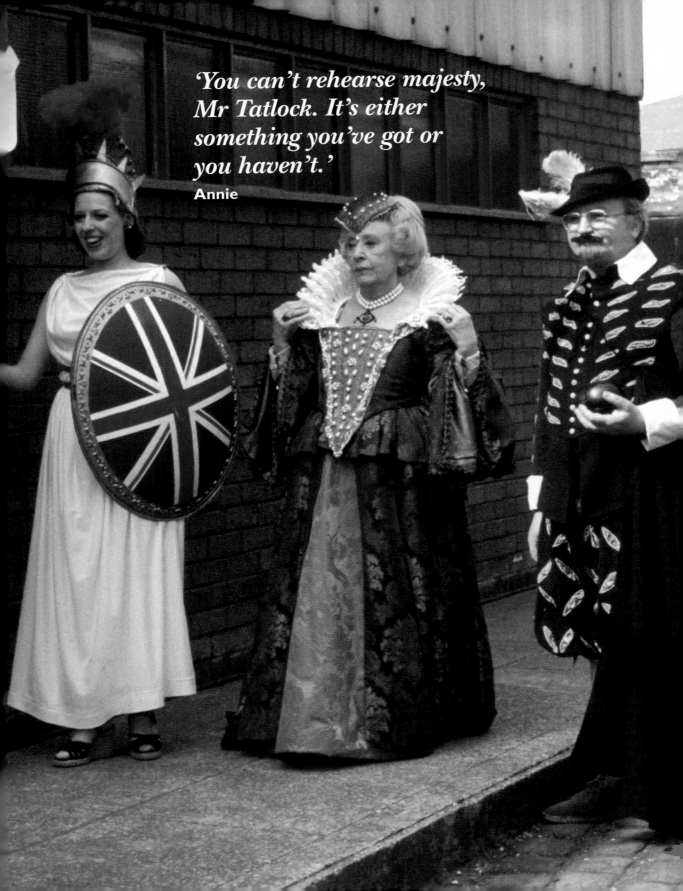

'You can't rehearse majesty, Mr Tatlock. It's either something you've got or you haven't.'
Annie

Queen of the Rovers

1977

Annie quashed Emily Bishop's ambitions to play Queen Elizabeth I on their 'Britain Through the Ages' Silver Jubilee float by explaining she'd already ordered the costume. Sealing the deal, she declared she'd also be happy to ask the brewery to provide a lorry, but only on the proviso that she played Queen Bess.

With Bet Lynch as Britannia, Ena Sharples as Queen Victoria and Fred Gee as Sir Francis Drake, everyone was ready for the parade – apart from the lorry, which refused to start. Initially downhearted, Annie felt responsible for the duff vehicle, but it turned out that Stan Ogden was to blame. Having left the lorry's lights on overnight to ensure no one stole it, the battery was now flat. The regulars banded together to determine his punishment – free drinks all round paid for by Stan!

'You've made a right muck of this. 'Ere, get me down off this lorry before it turns into a pumpkin.'
Ena

Do Not Feed The Spider.

Boris the Mexican Mouse-Eating Spider
1992

Hoping to lure more punters to the pub, Alec Gilroy rented Boris, a Mexican mouse-eating spider, from his mate Harry Norton who supplied animals for stage acts. All hell broke loose when Boris escaped from his container and made a reappearance crawling across the stove just as a health inspector arrived to give the premises the once over. Alec was left with only one possible course of action – to catch Boris in his hand and crush him. He later discovered there was no such thing as a Mexican mouse-eating spider.

1962 Boris wasn't the first exotic creature in the Rovers. The Walkers had the shock of their lives when they returned home from a brewery function to find three dancing girls in their bed and a pair of sea lions frolicking in the bath! Stuck for somewhere to put up his acts for the night, promoter Dennis Tanner had sneaked them in while they were out.

1983 Bet challenged the Rovers' beer-drinkers to lose weight and Eddie, Stan, Fred and Alf each agreed to put £5 each into a prize-fund kitty. Bet put Alf on a diet and Hilda refused to let Stan eat, but Fred was declared the winner after he lost a whopping five pounds. However, he was later disqualified when Bet revealed he'd cheated by putting bags of coins in his pockets at the 'before' weigh-in.

Up for the Challenge
1980

Despite being the one who'd accepted the barber-shop quartet sing-off challenge from landlord Tony Hayes at the Flying Horse, cellar-man Fred was promptly removed from the line-up for what could only be described as caterwauling. With nothing in the rules about the competitors having to be men, deep-voiced Renee Roberts stepped into the breach, complete with false moustache. But the Rovers' amateur trilling couldn't compete with the Flying Horse's vocal acrobatics and Renee, Alf, Bert and Eddie had to concede defeat.

Eyes on the Prize

2010

There was much excitement as the New Year's Eve charity raffle got underway – the first prize up for grabs was some saucy lingerie from Underworld, won by a bewildered Emily Bishop. Audrey Roberts nearly gagged at the thought of fingering Eddie Windass's toenails when he won a manicure and pedicure at her salon, but meanwhile rival hairdresser Claudia Colby had gone one further in the best prize stakes, offering a full cut and colour plus Indian head massage at her salon in the precinct – and much to Audrey's horror, she was holding the winning ticket. 'Oh for pity's sake,' she groaned from a booth. Claudia was determined to milk the moment. 'First time you've had a professional touch your barnet, eh Aud?' she cackled. 'Is it hair or is it a lampshade? I never can tell,' she mused to the regulars. 'I never know whether to talk to her or switch her on!'

2004

Pub cleaner Harry Flagg offered the first item at the charity Promise Auction and it was Blanche Hunt who snapped up the chance to have her nooks and crannies spring cleaned by his extendable feather duster.

Meanwhile Les Battersby offered himself as a slave for a day, which turned out to be his girlfriend Cilla's idea. 'None of this lot'll bid so I'll win him and then he'll be my slave. For a whole day I'll not let him out of the bedroom!' she salivated. But trashy Cilla hadn't bargained on a bidding war with Les' mischievous ex-wife Janice, who won him for £7.30. 'You're paying for Les Battersby?' asked a bewildered Eileen. Janice replied with a smirk. 'Have you seen that Cilla's face? Worth every penny...'

2004

Maudlin and drunk, Fred Elliott announced he'd donate a weekend in Paris to anyone who could prove romance still existed – although having sobered up the next day he quickly downgraded his offer to a stop-over at the Paris Hotel, Bridlington, instead. Kirk's attempt at a romantic gesture went pear-shaped when the tattooist etched 'I love Fez' instead of 'I love Fiz', Ken penned a soppy ode to Deirdre, but Ashley and Claire were declared the winners when she accepted his heartfelt marriage proposal in the pub.

Cover Stars

1978

There was much excitement when Newton & Ridley launched a new in-house magazine called *Over the Bar* and chose the Rovers as the perfect setting for the first issue's cover. Typically, Betty wasn't fussed about having her picture taken, whereas Annie insisted on regal-style posing and dolled-up Bet pouted and preened as if she was appearing in *Vogue*. When the magazine was published they were furious to see a much more relaxed Betty and the scruffy Eddie Yeats adorning the cover!

All Dressed Up
2006

Landlady Liz decided to liven up the pub's
New Year's Eve party with a fancy dress
theme – Stars of The Silver Screen. Barmaid
Violet came as Marilyn Monroe, Michelle
was a Kirsten Dunst-style cheerleader complete with
pom-poms and Liz was dressed soberly for once in a black waistcoat and
bowler hat. 'Oh Liz, you look fantastic. I love Stan Laurel,' enthused Michelle.
'I'm Sally Bowles,' she snapped back. Last to arrive was Sean, dressed as a
cowboy. 'Carry on Cowboy?' asked Violet. 'Brokeback Mountain...' he sighed.

   Steve had secretly set up the back room with candles and champagne
hoping to woo Michelle as the clock struck midnight, but he was gutted
to find her at the bar snogging love-rival Sonny. Meanwhile a delighted Liz
assumed the champagne and candles were from boyfriend Vernon. 'Oh my
Vern, have you done all this for me?' she gawped. 'Happy New Year, Tiger,' he
grinned, only too happy to take the glory.

Jumpers for Goalposts

2012

Ryan, Steve and Lloyd persuaded Stella to let them enter a five-a-side competition. When coach Lloyd picked the best of the bunch for the match against the Wethy Arms – Chesney, Paul, Ryan, Rob and Gary – he left Steve in a sulk when he failed to make the grade.

Even with hard taskmistress Stella taking a hands-on approach to training, the Rovers' team were unsure they'd be able to outwit the rival pub's giant goalie Barry the Gut Bucket. 'When he stands full on in that goal you'd be lucky to get a ping-pong ball past him,' sighed Lloyd.

When Gary pulled out, a desperate Lloyd turned to Steve to replace him. As predicted, they lost, then Rob goaded Steve, blaming his lack of fitness, and the pair scrapped on the pitch.

Eva: *'Are they honestly the best players you could find to represent the pub?'*
Stella: *'They're the cream of the crop.'*
Eva: *'If they're the cream of the crop I'd shoot the cow.'*

1995
Curly Watts signed up the Rovers for a five-a-side football league, but following a lacklustre performance in training he was dropped and replaced by a much sportier Nick Tilsley. The most exciting action happened off the pitch when spectator Phyllis Pearce was accosted by the Weatherfield Flasher – as he opened his raincoat she heroically beat him into submission with her handbag until he was arrested.

On the Pull

2010

Ciaran was chuffed when landlady Liz agreed to a speed-dating night, but Michelle was convinced he'd only suggested it to meet women himself. However, as the evening progressed Michelle began to soften towards the hunky barman and when Liz sent him out back for more glasses she told Michelle this was her chance to get him alone. But in the yard she was confronted by Ciaran with his lips glued to a leggy blonde he'd just pulled at the bar.

The next day the Irish charmer was full of himself because the event had been a success and Liz wanted him to come up with more theme nights. 'What next?' snapped Michelle. 'A stripper? Pole dancing?' Affronted, Ciaran insisted he would never be that trashy. 'Even when you've got your tongue down some lass's throat?' replied Michelle, peeved. Seeing his plan to make Michelle jealous had worked a treat, Ciaran flashed her his twinkliest smile. 'I'll change my ways if you go on a date with me. Save me, show me the light,' he pleaded. 'You do know this is borderline harassment?' she retorted, smiling despite herself.

> *'Speed dating is like fast food – instant gratification with a greasy aftertaste and a sense of deep regret...'*
> **Norris**

1983

As Bet viewed the men on offer at a video dating agency she nearly choked on her sherry when one of them turned out to be Jack Duckworth sporting a medallion, sipping a cocktail and claiming to be an entertainer called Vince St Clair. Playing him at his own game, Bet sent his wife Vera along to the agency, who arranged a date in the Rovers with 'Vince' under the pseudonym 'Carole Monroe'. Jack arrived to meet glamorous redhead Carole in the snug, but was

horrified to see his wife in a red wig snarling back at him. 'Well hello, Vince, terrific to meet ya!' she grimaced. As the regulars fell about laughing, a livid Vera chased Jack out of the pub, whacking him about the head with her clutch bag!

Kiss Me Quick
2001

As Geena's 'pound-a-kiss' charity night got underway, sometime-stripper Sam proved to be the biggest draw for the ladies and his expert lip-locking sent Edna all of a flutter. However a jealous Dev couldn't cope with the male population of Weatherfield queuing up to smooch his barmaid girlfriend. Taking matters into his own hands he pulled a crisp £50 pound note from his wallet. 'Fifty quid!' exclaimed Geena. 'What do you expect to get for that?' Dev replied: 'The next fifty kisses.' Smiling, Geena turned to the queue of puckered-up punters. 'Sorry boys,' she pouted. 'These lips are sealed!'

'Not bad, not bad at all. Pity he had a curry for his dinner...'

Edna on Sam

2011 Factory-worker Janice Battersby arrived at Singles Night dressed to kill in a low-cut scarlet top that left little to the imagination. Even Leanne muttered it was a bit daring. But Janice was loving all the attention. 'If you've got it, flaunt it!' she smirked as Gaz, a van driver from Underworld, asked her to join him for a drink at the bar. It turned out Gaz had a spare plane ticket to Tenerife for the next day and before you could say viva Espana, Janice had agreed to go with him. Leanne pulled her stepmother to one side, tutting she couldn't go away with someone she'd only just met. But a boozed-up Janice was beyond caring what anyone thought. 'Daz is a right laugh,' she slurred, happily. 'It's Gaz,' snapped Leanne.

RIVAL BOOZERS

You're never far from a Newton & Ridley pub in Weatherfield...

'You stand there smiling and simpering and coming the great I-am as usual, while all you really are is Lady Muck!'

Nellie to Annie

THE LAUGHING DONKEY

Nellie Harvey was Annie's equally snooty arch rival, who was convinced her premises (with a view of the park) were a cut above the grim environs of the Rovers. While the pair liked to keep up a fragile facade of friendship, their animosity knew no bounds in their attempts to outdo each other. But Annie played her ace when she was made Mayoress of Weatherfield – leaving poor Nellie green with envy. The following year Annie was horrified when Nellie's husband Arthur drunkenly declared his love for her, but she allowed him to sober up in Billy's room for the night. When Nellie arrived the next morning to find Arthur in pyjamas she convinced herself they were having an affair – and for the first time ever she told her rival exactly what she thought of her.

THE WEATHERFIELD ARMS

It was in the Wethy Arms that layabout Les Battersby first met barmaid Cilla Brown (she told him her name was Lulu, after the singer), who later became his wife. Liz also pulled pints there after she was forced out of the Rovers by Charlie Stubbs' lies. The current landlady is pouty vamp Carole Evans – a former employee of Stella Price who once had the hots for Karl.

THE QUEENS

Heralded as the jewel in the Newton & Ridley crown, both Bet and Stella Rigby seethed when their former employee Liz McDonald was given the keys to the much-admired pub.

'They've not barred anyone since Dick Turpin's time and then it was only his horse.'

Bet on the pub's clientele

Over the years the neighbouring alehouses have competed against each other in everything from darts matches and pram races to the infamous inter-pub Olympics. On Valentine's Day in 1999, Roy Cropper proposed to Hayley Patterson at a 70s night in the function room – and she accepted!

THE FLYING HORSE

'She might not be a fully paid-up member of the nymphomaniac club, but she definitely helps them out when they're shorthanded.'

Alec on Stella

Glamorous but scheming landlady Stella Rigby liked to lord it over Bet and her backstreet pub, but having both risen through the Newton & Ridley ranks, they soon realised they had a lot in common. In 1988 Alec was left fuming when newlywed Bet left him holding the fort while she holidayed in Morocco with Stella, because he'd been too stingy to shell out for a honeymoon.

THE WHITE SWAN

Bar Room Brawls

A magnet for bust-ups and booze-ups alike, if there's a fight brewing or a shouting-match in the offing, you can guarantee it'll come to a head in the Rovers. Where better to settle scores with a swift right hook or a pint hurled into the face than in the middle of a pub filled with your nearest and dearest. Get yourself a ringside seat by the bar and let the brawls begin...

Chavvy, am I? Chavvy? I'll give you chavvy!

Get your chavvy hands off me lady!

2008

Harry Mason's estranged wife Clarissa decided against divorcing the bookie after discovering he was having a fling with Liz. In the pub she baited the landlady about everything from her short skirts to her split-ends, before hurling a drink over her. Liz flipped and threw Clarissa out by her hair.

Clarissa: *'I wondered why you had such bad hands. Now I know. You wash 'em with soap.'*

Liz: *'I like to keep mine rough. Just so it really hurts when I slap ugly leeches right in the face.'*

Clarissa: *'They say you can tell a woman's age by her hands. But in your case it's the face.'*

Liz and Clarissa clash in the Ladies

2002

Rivals for the affections of barmaid Geena, Joe Carter and Dev's fisticuffs spilled out into the street. Appalled that Joe had thrown the first punch, Geena dumped him.

2011

Kylie taunted Tina about her boyfriend Graeme's fling with their Chinese friend Xin. When she sniggered, 'You Dim Sum you lose some!' it was the final straw for Tina, who launched herself at her.

2011

Gary blamed Sean when Izzy was mugged at a cashpoint on her secret night out with the camp bartender. Sean hit back with a few home truths and Gary lamped him one.

1961

When Elsie's husband Arnold turned up after 15 years asking for a divorce, Ena started muckraking that her neighbour had a mysterious new gentleman in tow. A slanging match followed as Elsie attempted to set the record straight.

Elsie: *'Shut up you. I'm warning you, if you don't learn to keep that flamin' lying gob of yours shut you're for the high jump!'*

Ena: *'Oh, nice language. Beautiful. Somebody never went to Sunday school. And what exactly am I supposed to have said?'*

Elsie: *'Is it true that you've been putting it around that I've been carrying on with a fella?'*

Ena: *'Well you are, aren't yer?'*

Elsie: *'Not that it's any of your business, but just for your information, that man happens to be my husband. It is my silver wedding next year and I also have my marriage lines to prove it ... more's the pity!'*

1980

After finding out that Bet had made a move on her new man, Elsie stormed into the Rovers and tussled with the unrepentant barmaid.

'If ever again you put your sticky fingers on any fella that belongs to me I'll knock your stupid peroxided head right off your silly shoulders!'

Elsie

2006

Drowning her sorrows after spending the night with her ex, Les, a bladdered Janice started poking fun at Sally by throwing peanuts at her. Sally shut her up with a right hook to the jaw!

2003

Shelley landed an almighty thwack on Peter when he revealed he was moving to Spain with Lucy. Then Lucy announced she'd been stringing him along to get her own back – she was going abroad without him and taking their son Simon.

1962

Elsie agreed to a date with married bookie Dave Smith in the Rovers, but Len jealously eyeballed them all evening. When Dave tried to warn him off, Len bashed him to the floor. The next day he received a summons for assault.

2007

On their wedding day Vernon caught fiancée Liz kissing her ex-husband Jim. Livid Vernon launched himself at him but didn't stand a chance against out-of-control Jim, who punched him to the ground.

'Are you seriously telling me that you want to marry a snivelling apology of a man like that one? No way, Elizabeth, you're mine!'

Jim

2012

After more goading from villainous Kirsty, barmaid Tina lost the plot and attacked her pregnant nemesis – and was later shunned by the shocked regulars.

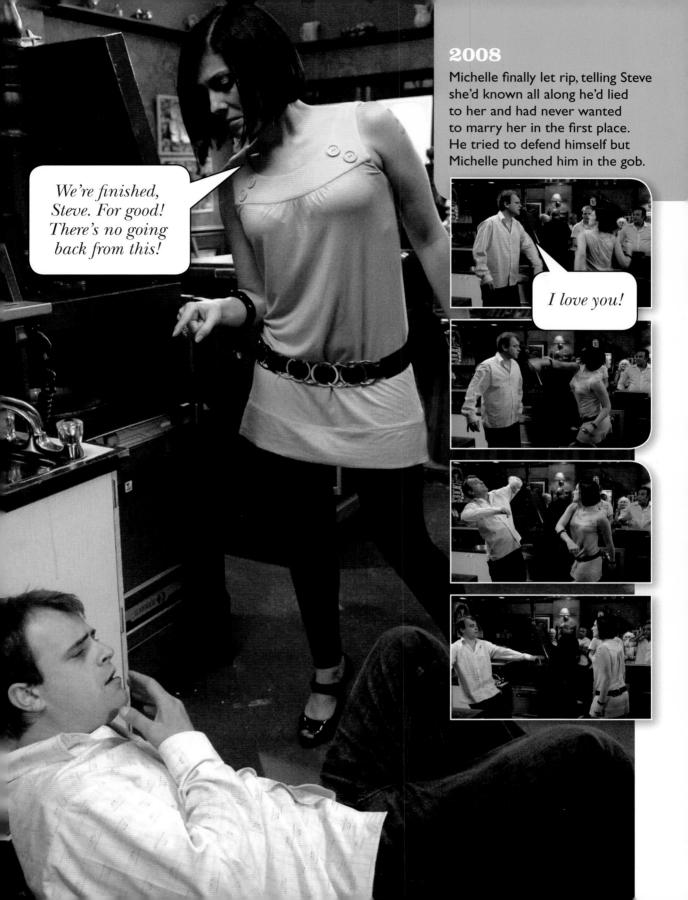

We're finished, Steve. For good! There's no going back from this!

2008

Michelle finally let rip, telling Steve she'd known all along he'd lied to her and had never wanted to marry her in the first place. He tried to defend himself but Michelle punched him in the gob.

I love you!

'What's happened to that strong, funny woman I used to know? I hardly recognise you these days!'

Sunita

2005

Shelley flew at Sunita when her friend hissed that Charlie had turned her into a pathetic shadow of her former self.

Come on then, Gobby Drawers – are you up for it? Outside now!

2009

Liz laughed in Teresa's face when she discovered the 'tragic slapper' had bedded Lloyd. Meanwhile Lloyd received a clout on the nose while trying to calm them down.

I decide when there's a fight in my pub … and I'm not scared of you, you rotten little cow!

I love her!

You love Kylie Minogue and Canal Street. You do not love her!

2012

Jason blew his top when Maria and Marcus announced they were an item – he whacked Marcus before Sean and Tommy pulled him away.

'*These two, they're seeing each other. The gay man and the fag hag have took it to a whole new level.*'

Jason

2010

On being released from jail, treacherous Tracy was confronted by her seething ex-cellmate Gail, who lunged at her.

You do it all with a big grin on your face. You don't give a second thought to the people you hurt, the pain and the misery you cause!

2010

Michelle threw a punch at Kylie for flirting with Ciaran, but Kylie ducked and it was Becky who ended up getting clobbered. When Becky sacked Michelle, Ciaran followed her out in disgust.

Kylie: *'Personally, I don't know how you can work behind there with him and not make a move.'*

Michelle: *'I would leave it there if I were you…'*

Kylie: *'Or maybe you have made a move and he knocked you back. That would explain that chewed-up face you're always wearing.'*

Kylie winds up Michelle

2005

After a day of taunts from Charlie about his fling with Bev, Ciaran finally blew his fuse and lunged for Shelley's twisted tormentor.

'A big bully who likes playing games with grown women. Bit different taking on someone your own size isn't it, scumbag!'

Ciaran

2009

Michelle snarled that Becky was a scrubber who was just after Steve's money when she discovered the pair were engaged. Michelle hurled a drink in her face and the rivals tussled, but at the last moment Becky held herself back from throwing a killer punch.

I am telling you now, lady, if you ever, ever try anything like that again, I will smash your smug little face in, do you understand?

2004

Unaware that newly returned Leanne was Nick's ex-wife, Maria informed her that apparently her boyfriend's ex was a right common tart. Later in the pub Leanne's identity was revealed and the pair fought like alley cats.

I can see I was right about you – you are common!

Have you looked in the mirror today? And you can stop with the Miss Congeniality bit. I know all about you. Nicking my sister's fella! She said you were a selfish whoring little cow and she was right!

2011

Events spiralled out of control at Jason Grimshaw's birthday party when Steve's estranged wife Becky took control behind the bar, much to the despair of newly installed manager Stella Price. Meanwhile Maria warned Carla off Frank Foster, her boyfriend Chris gave Frank a push, telling him to back off, and suddenly the whole pub had jumped into the fray. A horrified Steve returned from holiday to find a full-scale brawl taking place...

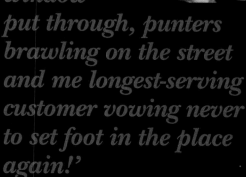

'I didn't expect to come back to find me window put through, punters brawling on the street and me longest-serving customer vowing never to set foot in the place again!'

Steve lets rip at Stella

Slaps!

Candice & Maria, 2003

Three days after being dumped by Nick, hairdresser Candice flipped when she discovered Maria had bedded him.

Bev & Charlie, 2005

On hearing that frightened Shelley had now taken to her bed, Bev stormed into the pub and whacked Charlie with all her might.

Stella & Eva, 2011

When she discovered Leanne was her half-sister, Eva called her mum a lying bitch, so Stella slapped her – and immediately regretted it.

Blanche & Ray, 1974

Yard secretary Deirdre was in tears thanks to the behaviour of big-headed builder Ray – so her no-nonsense mum Blanche walloped him in the Rovers.

Betty & Jack, 1998

After visiting hypnotherapist Magenta Savannah, Jack pretended to regress into a past life as eighteenth-century lothario 'Lusty Jack'. But when he pinched Betty's bum she wiped the smile of his face with a thunderous thwack.

> *Do you know why I love being a barmaid so much? 'Cos I can do this...*

A REFRESHING PINT

There's nothing like a face full of ale to liven up a night out at the Rovers...

2011
Realising her doctor boyfriend was embarrassed that she worked in a back-street boozer, Tina told Matt they were finished and chucked a pint over him when he tried to apologise.

2003
After a fall-out Maria aimed a pint at Bev, but she ducked and Shelley was saturated instead. Maria was promptly sacked.

1992

Jealous that he'd moved in fellow barmaid Raquel as his lodger, Angie chucked a beer over Des Barnes when he started boasting that women couldn't help but fall at his feet.

1988

When Gloria admitted she'd been bedding Sandra's boyfriend behind her back, the fuming Rovers' cleaner called her a tart and lobbed a pint at her.

1990

Curly Watts was chuffed to bits at being promoted to deputy manager at Bettabuys, but girlfriend Kimberley reckoned the power had gone to his head and drenched him.

2012

Tina blamed David when she was forced to announce to the pub that she was acting as a surrogate for Izzy and Gary — so she soaked him.

Hiya babe, I'm glad I've seen you. You know all that yesterday, me dumping you and everything. Well you're double dumped now — you lying cheat!

2006
Sarah Platt was hopping mad when she caught boyfriend Jason chatting to his ex, Violet, at the bar, so she threw a pint over his head and dumped him. The next day her rage escalated when she found out he'd proposed to Violet three weeks earlier — earning Jason a second soaking.

2001
Still furious that Dennis had left her for Janice, Eileen got revenge on her rival by spraying her with lager.

Janice: *'Look, we'd just like a drink.'*
Eileen: *'Well, you can have this one on me!'*

Revenge is best served cold? Well, there you go. Is that cold enough for you?

2003

On her first day as Underworld supervisor Karen enjoyed lording it over her former workmates – but Janice wasn't amused and later let her pint do the talking.

2010

On discovering Graeme had been wooing them both, Rosie and Natasha joined forces to get their own back. Natasha removed Graeme's hat while Rosie poured a pint over his head.

1994

In a bid to woo Fiona Middleton, Steve informed the hairdresser that he'd booked himself into the same Tenerife hotel as her. Furious that he'd ruined her holiday plans, she dumped his pint over his head.

2003

Boasting she could have any man she wanted, temptress Tracy attempted to pull Roy. A furious Hayley decided against hurling a pint and opted to sling the contents of an ice-bucket over her instead.

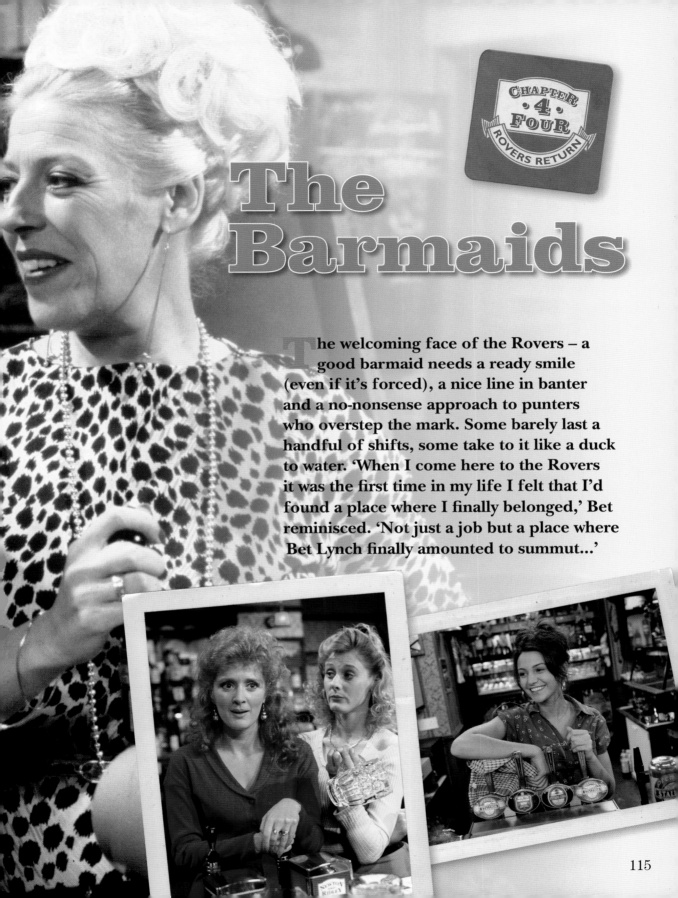

The Barmaids

The welcoming face of the Rovers – a good barmaid needs a ready smile (even if it's forced), a nice line in banter and a no-nonsense approach to punters who overstep the mark. Some barely last a handful of shifts, some take to it like a duck to water. 'When I come here to the Rovers it was the first time in my life I felt that I'd found a place where I finally belonged,' Bet reminisced. 'Not just a job but a place where Bet Lynch finally amounted to summut...'

Concepta Riley
1960–1963

Concepta was down-to-earth and kind-hearted, the Walkers adored her and she became one of Annie's closest confidantes. But despite her best efforts to appease Ena Sharples, the grim-faced stout-drinker would often rudely refer to her as 'that Paddy'. Much to the Walkers' disappointment, Concepta quit the Rovers in October 1961 to marry bus inspector Harry Hewitt, who didn't approve of her working in the pub. However, later, when strapped for cash, she returned to bar work.

Nona Willis

1961

On her first night behind the bar the glamorous Cockney was told in no uncertain terms by an unsmiling Ena that Londoners were not welcome on her street. Ena took further offence when it was revealed Nona had once been an exotic dancer. Fortunately for Ena, Nona handed in her notice after a month, explaining she found it difficult to understand the customers' Northern accents.

Doreen Lostock

1961

Ditzy Doreen left Elliston's Raincoats to work behind the bar, but her heart wasn't in it and after a spell on the Gamma Garments shop floor, she surprised everyone by joining the Women's Royal Army Corps.

Irma Ogden
1964–1965

Irma's first shift didn't start well when she accidentally smashed Annie's willow-patterned plate. In a panic she tried to glue the pieces back together, but to her surprise the landlady thanked her for breaking the platter as she hadn't liked it in the first place. Annie did later sack (but eventually reinstated) Irma on discovering she had let her wheeler-dealer brother Trevor stash 12 sacks of dodgy onions in the cellar.

Lucille Hewitt
1968–1974

The Walkers' surrogate daughter took on occasional shifts at the pumps after her stepmum Concepta and dad Harry emigrated to Ireland. Jack and Annie attempted to give moral guidance to their lively young ward but Lucille kept them on their toes. She told Annie she'd landed a job as a receptionist at the YWCA but was actually working as a go-go dancer at the Aquarius disco club under the stage name Lita Laverne.

Emily Nugent
1968–1970

The meek and mild Emily felt obliged to occasionally help out when she lodged at the Rovers but she never really felt at home behind the bar. She proved to be surprisingly assertive, refusing to serve a band of unruly builders (who kept pinching her bottom) until they behaved like gentlemen. But the Mission Hall church committee objected to their secretary working in a back-street boozer and so Emily pulled her last pint.

'I've just never seen myself sleeping a rafter away from a public bar. They still tend to be rudely male, don't they?'

Emily's unsure about moving in

Bet Lynch
1970–1985

Len Fairclough once commented that 'Her and those pumps go together like Morecambe and Wise', and from barmaid to landlady, the Rovers is where Bet belonged.

Blonde, brassy and bold, Bet was a grafter who'd had a tough upbringing and was determined to better her lot in this world. Her mother struggled to bring her up alone after her dad abandoned them when she was six months old. Pregnant at just 16, Bet felt forced to give up her son for adoption and 19 years later she found out he'd been killed in a car crash. While her love life lurched from one disaster to the next and included unsuitable suitors such as Len, Mike Baldwin and even Jack Duckworth, her love for the Rovers never wavered.

But it hadn't started off well. Annie took an instant dislike to her son Billy's choice of new recruit, convinced her slinky black mini-dress and bare shoulders were lowering the tone. Annie ordered Billy to get rid. 'Would you mind telling Miss Lynch to get dressed and go home? I will not have the standard of this pub lowered to something more suitable for the dock road!'

But Billy stood his ground and soon it was obvious the bombshell with the beehive was an asset, profits were soaring and a Rovers' legend was born.

'Me behind a bar, I'm in me element. It's like Santa Claus in his grotto.
Bet

Suzie Birchall
1983

Gail's man-eating best friend returned to Weatherfield after three years 'Down South' and landed a job as barmaid. Suzie won Annie's admiration by refusing to have a row with Vera when the redhead was accused of flirting with her hubby Jack. Unfortunately she wasn't so restrained with Gail's husband, Brian, and disappeared after a failed attempt to seduce him.

Kath Goodwin
1984

The divorcée found herself in the crossfire when ladies' man and temporary manager Frank Harvey asked both her and Bet to be his date at the brewery ball. Opting for a quiet life, Kath quit the Rovers after only one week. Meanwhile, to get her own back on Frank, Bet turned up at the ball dressed as a tramp.

Maureen Barnett
1985

Sensible-shoed Maureen was Betty's old friend brought in to help out at the pub, but was left holding the fort while Frank Harvey wooed (and bedded) another new recruit, Gloria Todd.

Gloria Todd

1985–1988

On becoming landlady Bet dispensed with Gloria's services, stating she didn't have enough experience. Furious but undeterred, the younger barmaid went away to learn her trade before returning to the Rovers and managing to impress Bet.

Bet and Gloria became firm friends and shared a history of doomed relationships. Gloria's flirtation with barman Frank Mills turned violent, two-timing psycho Alan Bradley was cheating on her with Rita and, although she was smitten with Mike Baldwin, he was just using her as a cover for his affair with a married woman. Gloria got her hopes up when she received roses, but was crushed to discover her secret admirer was married pot-man Jack.

She left the Rovers in 1988 after falling for Pete Shaw, the boyfriend of cleaner Sandra Stubbs, who threw a pint over Gloria and called her a tart when the truth came out.

Sally Seddon
1986

Betty was unhappy when Kevin's fiancée started pulling pints, saying she was too hard-faced. Sally walked out a few weeks later when Bet cut her hours.

Alison Dougherty
1986

Bubble-permed Alison was recruited after the Rovers' fire but within days Bet's crafty rival Alec Gilroy had lured her to work behind the bar of his Graffiti Club. However, Bet had the last laugh when light-fingered Alison did a runner with the club's takings!

Margo Richardson
1987

While Bet holidayed in Spain, Alec finally managed to force his old adversary Betty out of the pub. He took feisty Margo on as her replacement, but once again Bet swooped to the rescue, sacked Margo and brought back her beloved Betty.

Tina Fowler
1989–1990

After winning Newton & Ridley's Barmaid of the Month competition Tina secretly began dating brewery supremo Nigel Ridley. Soon big-headed Tina began slacking off and then barred regular Percy Sugden because she was bored by his long-winded stories. A furious Bet sacked her and took great delight in chucking her out.

Liz McDonald
1990–1996, 2000–2001, 2004, 2006

Liz worked at the bookies and as Diggory Compton's bakery assistant, but pubs were in her blood. She served at the Queens, the Weatherfield Arms, the Legion, as well as many stints at the Rovers. It was a dream come true when Liz finally became landlady of the Coronation Street pub in 2006, but the path that took her there had been a rocky one.

In 1992, after losing her baby Katie who was born prematurely, Liz took some time off and was assured by Bet she could always have her old job back. But when she tried to return, Alec said she was too old and a furious Liz took a job at the Legion.

In 1993 she had made such a success of temporarily running the Rovers that the brewery agreed to take her and husband Jim on as trainee managers at the Queens, Newton & Ridley's most prized pub. But her tenure ended in tears when an increasingly volatile Jim accused her of sleeping with brewery boss Richard Willmore and thumped him.

In 2004, after being on the receiving end of Charlie Stubbs' sleazy come-ons, she tried to warn manager Shelley her boyfriend had a dark side – but Shelley refused to believe her, calling her an old trollop before throwing her out of the pub.

'Big hair, short skirt and fella trouble … it can only be Liz McDonald.'

Bet

Angie Freeman

1991–1992

Fashion designer and part-time barmaid Angie was raging when boyfriend Des Barnes invited leggy Raquel Wolstenhulme to move in as his lodger. In the pub Des boasted he couldn't help it if he had women falling at his feet, so Angie poured a pint over his head and resigned. When she later discovered Raquel had taken her job at the pub, she threw her shoes at her, saying she might as well have them too!

Raquel Wolstenhulme
1992–1996

She was a wide-eyed natural behind the bar but as Raquel often pointed out, she was a model by profession, a barmaid out of necessity. But the dizzy pint-puller, who failed to be crowned Miss Bettabuy (North West Division), never saw her modelling career take off. She had an assignment modelling knitting patterns and slippers (although her feet were too big) but then her agency went bust owing her £500.

Ever the optimist, Raquel signed up at the Mayfair Modelling Academy in Croydon (using the more alluring name of Nadia) and was thrilled to be offered a shoot for designer brand Armani. But the address she'd been given was to a shop called 'R. Marney: High Class Fruit and Veg'. She'd been tricked by fellow barmaid Tanya Pooley, who was vying with Raquel for the affections of local bookie, Des Barnes.

Eventually Raquel settled for a marriage of convenience with Curly Watts, but when new landlady Vera fired her to make room for son Terry to work behind the bar, Raquel retrained as an aromatherapist. She was then offered the chance of a job in Kuala Lumpur, which she took, leaving behind a broken-hearted Curly.

'It's one thing I'm grateful to my mother for, calling me Raquel. It may sound like a brand of disinfectant, but at least nobody shortens it.'
Raquel

> *'I'm the bitchy type, the manipulating type, the home-breaking type. I'm surprised you haven't heard about me.'*
> **Tanya**

Tanya Pooley
1993–1994

Tanya had worked at the Queens where she did her very best to destroy the McDonalds' marriage. She was the master of manipulation and bitchy put-downs, and Bet didn't know what she was letting herself in for when she gave her a job. Tanya hated Raquel on sight and went on a date with her fellow barmaid's ex, Des, purely out of spite. But her crowing about sending Raquel on a bogus modelling assignment backfired when Des brought a tearful Raquel home and the pair spent the night together. When Raquel asked her why she'd done such a nasty thing, Tanya was her usual brusque self: 'Because I'm sick and tired of you looking down your nose at the rest of us, going on about how you're not a real barmaid, you're really a model. What you really are, luv, is an over-made-up tart. And that's all you'll ever be, so you'd better get used to it.'

She delighted in telling a devastated Raquel she'd slept with Des and later announced to the pub that Raquel had been thrown off her modelling course. Enough was enough and a protective Bet fired her. In a final act of revenge, Tanya bedded Bet's trucker boyfriend Charlie Whelan and wasted no time sharing the news of her latest devastating conquest.

Jenny Bradley
1993

Rita's former foster daughter reappeared in Weatherfield after she claimed she'd been dumped by her married lover and a sympathetic Bet gave her a job at the Rovers. However, when it became clear the only thing Jenny was interested in was getting her hands on Rita's savings, Rita threw her out for good.

Joyce Smedley
1996–1997

The cash-strapped Rovers' cleaner had the hots for Alec and occasionally helped out behind the bar (see page 223).

Carol Starkey
1995

Misery guts Carol didn't even finish her trial shift before asking to be paid off by Jack – complaining the customers were too depressing.

Lorraine Ramsden
1995

Jack was so enamoured with his potential new employee that he didn't even bother to interview her. It turned out Lorraine couldn't even pull a pint and when Vera returned from holiday to find Jack giving the curvy blonde a cosy one-on-one tutorial in pump action, Lorraine was swiftly given the boot.

Samantha Failsworth
1996–1998

Motorbike-riding Samantha caused mayhem after she roared into the Street and charmed Jack and Vera into giving her a job. Separated from her husband, she developed a friendship with Curly and had an intense on-off relationship with Des. When she discovered her ex, Des (who she'd been two-timing anyway), was dating fellow barmaid Natalie Horrocks, she started a sinister campaign to split them up. She told Des she was pregnant with his baby and was going to have an abortion. He was devastated and begged her not to, but she later claimed she'd had a miscarriage anyway.

She also faked a phone call from the hospital saying Natalie's son Tony had been in an accident and then she kidnapped Natalie's cat, Tiger. She sobbed feebly on Alec's shoulder claiming Des was pestering her, as she played everyone off against each other. Finally, when confronted by her victims she admitted all her dastardly deeds but refused to show any remorse and instead, as a cruel parting shot, teased Des that she really was pregnant with his child after all.

> '*You're just some sad little girl who likes messing up people's lives.*'
> **Natalie**

Judy Mallett
1996–1997, 1999

Mouthy Judy blasted her way in to Weatherfield when she gave the Duckworths a gob-full after her husband Gary was electrocuted by the faulty wiring in the house they'd just sold them. This led to the Malletts being banned from the Rovers for life, but eventually both sides mellowed and Judy juggled her job at the amusement arcade with shifts at the pub and became a popular figure behind the bar despite an initial fall-out with fellow barmaid Samantha. When her twins William and Rebecca were born, it was a kind-hearted Vera who bought their christening gowns as she knew the couple couldn't afford to buy their own.

But months later tragedy struck and Judy collapsed while pegging out washing in the backyard. She'd suffered an embolism brought on by a car accident a few weeks earlier.

'She's got a lovely face. It's a shame about what comes out of her mouth.'

Mavis

137

Leanne Tilsley
1999–2000, 2008, 2012

When teenager Leanne landed in the Rovers, she brought trouble with her. On one of her shifts, two masked thugs stormed the bar, knocked her to the floor, unconscious, and stole money from the till. She was hailed a heroine but, consumed by guilt, she later admitted to landlady Natalie the raid had been a set-up and she'd known about it all along. She was a cocaine addict and had been forced into the plan by scary gangster drug-dealer Jez Quigley. Natalie was outraged, but relented when a repentant Leanne agreed to attend drug counselling.

After burning down her Italian restaurant as part of an insurance scam, Leanne returned to bar work in 2008, but was sacked by a paranoid Michelle Connor who was convinced she was having an affair with Steve McDonald. The pair scrapped like alley cats on the cobbles but despite Michelle apologising the next day, Leanne told her where she could stick her job.

Leanne: *'I've got booze runnin' through my veins, me.'*
Natalie: *'That doesn't surprise me with Les Battersby as yer dad…'*

Geena Gregory
2000–2002

When Duggie Ferguson took over as landlord he assured Geena she would be his second in command, so she was seething when his old pal Shelley Unwin was given the position. When the pub was put up for sale Geena was determined she and boyfriend Dev Alahan would buy it, but her rival Shelley and her other half Peter Barlow had the same idea.

On the day of the auction they were all pipped at the post by Fred Elliott, who gave the job of temporary manageress to Shelley. A sulky Geena worked to rule and purposefully didn't tell Shelley they were out of tonic, which led to Fred questioning Shelley's abilities. Shelley was furious when her rival pinched her idea for the Rovers' centenary party and after an almighty row Geena walked out. Eventually she was persuaded to return and the pair continued to tiptoe around each other.

Geena's world was about to be turned upside down when she discovered fiancé Dev had bedded Deirdre Rachid. On the rebound she fell into the arms of manipulative wide-boy Joe Carter, which led to a huge fight in the Rovers (see page 96).

Amy Goskirke
2000

After arriving in Weatherfield to manage his Uncle Ravi's shop, Dev Alahan was less than overjoyed to discover ex-girlfriend Amy had followed him up from Birmingham and bagged a job in the Rovers. His lack of enthusiasm was understandable when it became clear that Amy was an unhinged fantasist. She falsely claimed to be expecting his baby and then faked her own suicide-bid. Only when Dev pulled off her bandages to reveal her wrists had not been slashed was she finally exposed as a deranged liar.

Toyah Battersby
2000–2001

The keen journalism student lodged at the pub with Natalie, working part-time behind the bar. After a night out Toyah was walking down the alleyway at the back of the Rovers when she was grabbed from behind, pulled to the floor and raped. Her motionless, bruised body was found by teenager Jason Grimshaw. Over the next few weeks, traumatised by her ordeal and having never actually seen the face of her assailant, Toyah began to suspect all the male residents including Jason, garage mechanic Sam Kingston and fellow pub employee Peter Barlow. Eventually a DNA test proved her attacker had been Phil Simmonds, a friend who'd pretended to support and care for her.

> '*We pull pints, we smile at the punters and we put money in tills. We do not clean lavs, lift crates or do wonders with a piece of scrag-end.*'
>
> **Shelley lays down the law to Fred**

Shelley Unwin
2001–2006

Having pulled pints at the rowdy rugby club, the Rovers was a breeze for no-nonsense Shelley. But within minutes of her arrival she'd managed to upset both Betty and Edna by slamming the standard of the hotpot and the cleaning. She also irritated Geena by ordering her around and managed to get Peter Barlow sacked after spotting him helping himself to whisky. She felt guilty about this and soon the pair were dating.

Meanwhile new boss Fred admitted he'd been impressed with the way she'd run the Rovers on a temporary basis and took her on as permanent manager. She subsequently married Peter and life was looking rosy. That was until it turned out her new husband was a two-timing bigamist (see page 205).

Edna Miller
2001

The gloomy cleaner persuaded Duggie to give her a trial behind the bar, but she quit after one shift, complaining the service-with-a-smile rule was too much of a strain.

Eve Sykes
2001

Eve was an unlikely romantic interest for Fred considering it was Eve's son Dean who'd held him at gunpoint during the Freshco siege. His friends and family were convinced Eve was a gold-digger, just like her daughter Linda Baldwin, but Fred was smitten. Having lost her job at the Turk's Head she was chuffed when Duggie offered her work at the Rovers, unaware it was only because Fred was secretly paying her wages. They married at a posh country house hotel, but Eve later fled when Fred discovered she was a bigamist.

Maria Sutherland
2002–2003

Audrey refused to give Maria her job back at the hair salon on the grounds of family loyalty after learning she'd walked out on boyfriend Nick in Canada. Shelley then took on the grateful Maria at the Rovers instead.

Bev Unwin

2003–2004, 2005–2006

Shelley's mum's highly-strung nerves were made even worse by her choice of men. She had a drunken one-night stand with toyboy chef Ciaran McCarthy (although she would've liked it to have been a more regular pairing) and was also seduced by Shelley's villainous boyfriend Charlie Stubbs. Unable to bear the guilt, she confessed all to a dumbfounded Shelley. Charlie confidently lied his way out of it and implied Bev was obsessed with him, resulting in Shelley turfing out her mum.

As Charlie's manipulative hold over Shelley tightened, an increasingly worried Bev feared for her daughter's safety, even offering Charlie £100,000 to leave Shelley alone, which he smugly declined. To her immense relief, Shelley jilted the bully boy builder and Bev moved on with her life, which included getting engaged to Fred. But Bev wasn't to get her happy-ever-after when Fred died of a stroke on the morning of their wedding at the home of his ex, Audrey Roberts.

'You throw yourself at men, make a complete fool of yourself and then sit round licking your wounds like an embittered cat. You can't bear to see anyone being happy because you're so washed up and pathetic!'

Shelley

Tracy Barlow

2003, 2011

Shelley immediately regretted taking Tracy on as a favour to her fiancé Peter as it was clear his lazy stepsister was more interested in helping herself to free drinks and gossiping with the punters than helping out behind the bar. Tracy lasted one whole day before being given her marching orders.

In 2011 Steve offered his ex another stint at the pub in a last-ditch attempt to stop her leaving Weatherfield with his daughter Amy. Tracy began a campaign to reunite herself with Steve, resulting in his wife Becky losing the plot completely and smashing up Ken and Deirdre's house with a sledgehammer.

In an attempt to win their custody battle, Steve used Tracy's own cheating tactics by leading her to believe that with Becky out of the way, they could become a proper family and run the Rovers together. Instead, Steve duped Tracy into signing an access agreement without reading it. Then with a big grin on his face he told an incandescent Tracy he no longer required her services and she was sacked!

'*Winding people up is her favourite hobby. If she went on Mastermind her specialist subject'd be Winding People Up: 1977 to 2012.*'

Steve

Violet Wilson
2004–2008

Violet was a former pupil of Ken Barlow, who she insisted on calling 'sir' when she served him. She was instantly smitten with builder Jason Grimshaw but ended it when she discovered he'd been having an affair with Sarah Platt. In 2007, Violet, who was worried about her fertility, and her gay best friend, Sean Tully, who was worried about never having a child of his own, made a pact to try for a baby together while she was on a break from boyfriend Jamie. The plan resulted in a boy called Dylan who was born in the Rovers (see page 191).

Fred: *'A gem is what she is, now let her shine. She comes to us festooned with praise.'* **Shelley:** *'From who? Landlords who wanted shut of her?'*

Lauren Wilson
2007–2008

Violet's freeloading little sister turned up in Weatherfield, blagged herself a job at the Rovers and proceeded to grab attention, cause trouble and run up debts. The locals heaved a sigh of relief when she went on holiday to Tenerife with Sean and never came back.

147

Michelle Connor
2006–2010, 2013–

It was a lecherous Vernon who recommended Michelle, a glossy-haired singer in his band, be hired as a barmaid. Fred agreed, much to a jealous Liz's fury. But Steve McDonald had his sights set on Michelle from the word go and over the years they've enjoyed a lengthy on/off romantic relationship despite her flings with Ciaran McCarthy, Peter Barlow and bisexual Sonny, and Steve having married both volatile Becky and demonic Tracy.

Deirdre: *'Wonder how she gets her hair so shiny?'* **Liz:** *'Dunno…probably combs it with a pork chop.'*

Kelly Crabtree
2008

The brash factory girl surprised her fellow machinists when she tottered towards them from behind the bar and started serving. 'Since when were you a barmaid?' asked Sean. 'Erm, since about 30 seconds ago when Liz asked me to do a few shifts,' she replied, at the start of her one and only shift.

Poppy Morales
2008–2009

After meeting the strong-willed Poppy at her Brazilian Crunch keep-fit classes, Liz took her on as assistant manager. But after criticising Betty's tea-breaks, time-keeping and then leaving her off the rota completely, Poppy's attitude was seen as too abrasive for the Rovers. Steve managed to secure Betty's return and wife Becky secured Poppy's departure by throwing her out of the pub – by her hair!

'Here's the thing, you're a bossy two-faced cow and nobody wants you here. So unless you want that as your reference I suggest you sling yer hook right now.'

Becky sacks Poppy

Becky Granger
2008–2011

It was Michelle who offered reformed bad girl Becky her first shift, little knowing Becky had already enjoyed a night of passion with her other half Steve. Eventually Becky and Steve went public with their relationship and a furious Michelle poured a drink over Becky's head to congratulate them. The couple finally got married at the second attempt but Becky was arrested during their celebrations in the pub and spent her wedding night in a prison cell (see page 198).

'I'm not a crier, me. I sat there hard-faced through the whole of ET.'

Becky

Sunita Alahan
2012

Relieved to escape Dev and the corner shop, Sunita became friends with landlady Stella Price who gave her a bed and a job at the Rovers. She repaid her new pal by embarking on an affair with her partner Karl. Their fling was exposed when Stella came home early one night to find them grappling in a booth in the pub.

Mandy Kamara
2012–2013

Mandy was an ex of Lloyd's who had kept his daughter Jenna a secret from him. The couple decided to make a fresh start, and when Mandy's great culinary skills were revealed, Stella took her on to share the cooking duties with an overworked Sean Tully. However, Sean remained protective of Betty's prized hotpot recipe and an amused Mandy agreed to keep quiet about its secret ingredients. When Lloyd and Mandy's reunion faltered, she left Weatherfield and the Rovers with no hard feelings.

Tina McIntyre
2010–

Former Kabin assistant Tina had barely served her first pint in the Rovers when a tram ploughed off the viaduct and ripped through the street – she panicked, believing her boyfriend Graeme Proctor was trapped in the flat above the destroyed corner shop, but he turned up safe and sound. The couple split when Graeme's sham marriage to their Chinese friend Xin blossomed into a real relationship, but Tina later found solace in the arms of mechanic Tommy Duckworth and was amused when he was forced into the Rovers in only his boxer shorts after a prank by Rosie Webster.

Tina was the first to spot Tyrone's new girlfriend Kirsty was a wrong 'un and was shunned by the regulars when a scuffle with the pregnant ex-cop ended in a fall and Kirsty going into labour in the pub. Tina herself went into labour with her surrogate baby Jake during the reopening party after the fire. (see page 193).

Eva Price
2012

Eva moved into the Rovers shortly after her mother, Stella, announcing she'd cancelled her wedding because of her cheating fiancé. Eva's mood didn't improve when she discovered that the reason for the move to Weatherfield was to track down her secret half-sister Leanne. Eva fell for bistro owner Nick but it wasn't mutual and she was gutted when she lost her bloke and her job in one day. She helped out at the Rovers before working at Underworld as a machinist, but just when she thought her year couldn't get any worse, Nick admitted he was in love with her sister Leanne, leaving a bitter and downhearted Eva doing her utmost to ruin their wedding.

'I should apologise for my daughter, something I do quite often. I toyed with the idea of getting it printed on a t-shirt to save me opening me gob.'
Stella

Gloria Price
2012–2013

Stella's melodramatic mother turned up unexpectedly from Spain, insisting she needed to lie low as she was on the run from gangsters who had dodgy business dealings with her rich boyfriend Clifford. This all proved to be a figment of her vivid imagination and, rather than living on the Costa del Crime, she'd actually worked at a dry-cleaners which she'd accidentally burnt down, leaving her destitute.

Gloria clearly loved a drama and lied to Lewis Archer, claiming to be terminally ill with cancer in a hare-brained scheme to expose him as a conman. She then faked the results of the Pub of the Year competition, naming herself as landlady and barring Norris Cole after finding his uncomplimentary note in the anonymous comments box.

Fed up with her mother's games, Stella kicked her out, but the following year Gloria reappeared with a moneybags fiancé, Eric Babbage, in tow. When Eric dropped dead in a booth, Stella softened towards her mother and agreed Gloria could move into the Rovers on the condition she turned over a new leaf.

'Following the arrival of new staff in recent weeks the quality of service has deteriorated ... and the landlady's mother is vulgar and loud.'

Gloria reads Norris's comments card

Being Betty

Larger-than-life landladies, buxom barmaids and loyal punters may have come and gone, but no-nonsense hotpot queen (and occasional dart-playing hot shot) Betty remained the real treasure behind the bar of the Rovers for over 40 years. This incredible achievement saw her crowned Weatherfield's Oldest Serving Barmaid in 2010 – even though at one point she thought she'd killed off her nearest competitor with a dodgy hotpot. The indispensable, straightforward and wise Betty had an eventful time at the Rovers, returning so many times after being sacked or stomping out in a huff, she may as well have had her own revolving door...

'The secrets I've had to keep working here. I tell yer, I could get in MI5 with my qualifications.'

Betty

1969

Betty arrives to help run her sister Maggie Clegg's corner shop. Jack Walker takes her on at the Rovers, but Annie takes an instant dislike to plain-speaking Betty and fires her for reasons of incompatibility. Betty refuses to accept the decision and carries on working. Forced into a corner, Jack gives her a week's notice. Humiliated, Betty flounces out. The next day Annie apologises and Betty returns.

1969

Annie falsely accuses Betty and Hilda of stealing a necklace. Furious at being slandered, Betty walks out. She takes a job at the Flying Horse, but is persuaded to come back.

1970

Betty is annoyed when Annie allows Bet to have Christmas off. She's won round when Annie suggests they call her Elizabeth from now on, whereas the younger barmaid would remain common old Bet.

1974

Betty's husband Cyril dies and it's revealed that Gordon, who has been raised by Maggie as her own, is in fact Betty's illegitimate son.

1975

Betty's chuffed to win Newton & Ridley's Personality of the Pub competition.

1976

Annie informs the barmaids they'll have to take a pay cut due to the recession. Betty stages a walk-out in protest.

1977

Annie accuses Betty of stealing £45 from her sewing basket – again, she storms out.

1981

Relief manager Gordon Lewis suspends Fred and so Betty and Bet walk out in protest. Betty gets a job at the Rifleman, but returns on the proviso that she'll run the pub in Annie's absence in future.

1982

She's shocked when old flame Ted Farrell visits out of the blue. He's Gordon's father but she doesn't tell him.

1983

Betty gives drunken Fred the silent treatment when he says she's got a fat backside, but she later walks out when he makes light of Gordon's illegitimacy.

1984

Fred refuses to take orders from Betty when Annie leaves her in charge. He secretly contacts the brewery, who make him temporary manager, much to her fury.

1986

Feeling too old for bar work she retires after the fire, but she soon gets itchy feet and returns to cook the food.

1989

Tired of being caught in the middle of the Gilroys' marriage problems, Betty resigns but later returns when the couple are reconciled.

1987

Alec tries to force her out by making her do cellar work. Fed up with being treated like a skivvy, Betty retires (again). She comes out of retirement to help Bet while Alec is laid up with the flu.

1992

Alec has Betty in tears when he explains her services are no longer required as the kitchen is too outdated for food preparation. But Bet steps in and makes Alec cough up for new catering equipment.

'There's no getting rid of her, is there? She should be written into the deeds of this place.'

Alec fails to sack Betty

1994

After his wife Audrey quits in a huff, Betty is delighted when Mayor Alf Roberts asks her to be his Mayoral consort. She becomes Mayoress for his remaining five months in office.

1995

At the pub's VE Day commemoration party Betty recognises one of the old soldiers as her first love, Billy Williams. They marry and on returning from their honeymoon she's stunned to discover Vera Duckworth is her new boss. She resigns when Vera orders her to clean as well as cook. But Vera can't cope without her and Betty negotiates lunch shifts and complete control of the kitchen as part of her reinstatement.

1996

The Duckworths leave Betty in charge while they go on holiday, but on their return they accuse her of fiddling the books. She storms out. It later transpires takings had been up under her management.

1997

Alec gleefully writes Betty a letter of dismissal when she fails to turn up for work. He then finds out Billy has died of a heart attack, so he quickly retrieves the unopened envelope from her letterbox. Vera comforts her, saying she has a job for life.

1998

Mischievous Jack pretends to be under the spell of a hypnotist and grabs Betty's backside – in response she wallops him across the face.

1999

She grudgingly agrees to cover an evening shift and is delighted to be surprised with a party celebrating her 30th anniversary at the Rovers.

2000

Betty walks out on hearing Natalie's plans to sell to the Boozy Newt chain. However, new co-owner Mike Baldwin persuades her to return, but only after she wrangles a pay rise and a holiday.

2001

She's thrilled to receive a lifetime achievement award from Newton & Ridley.

'You have to admire the old bird. Nothing gets her down. You know I've heard she's indestructible, like Captain Scarlet. You can fire bullets at her, set her on fire and nothing. Bullets just bounce off her.'

Ciaran on Betty

2002

Betty decides to move to London to be with her son, Gordon. Fred Elliott arranges a surprise retirement party and for her old pal Bet to be there. However she's soon back in Weatherfield and agreeing to help out a short-staffed Shelley.

2004

Betty storms out of the pub following a row with newly-promoted manager Bev Unwin, but returns after lots of grovelling from Fred.

2009

After celebrating 40 years of service, Betty realises she's been sacked by new manageress Poppy Morales when her name is missed off the rota. Owner Steve successfully begs her to return.

2010

Betty is crowned the oldest serving barmaid in Manchester, but she almost kills Enid Crump, a rival to the title, by serving her an out-of-date hotpot. She's relieved to discover Enid has survived and that her sudden illness had been due to the large amount of port she'd consumed.

2012

Gordon arrives to break the terrible news that Betty has died in her sleep. The residents gather to show their respect as her hearse is driven down the cobbles. As for her wake, where else could it have been but at the Rovers...

Hotpot Heaven

Not even Betty Williams herself, the creator of the legendary meaty dish, could remember when she served her very first hotpot, but over the years the pub grub that bears her name has become a Rovers' institution and her recipe a closely guarded secret.

Management and co-workers have tried to interfere in the preparation of her signature dish, but none have succeeded. She gave money-grabbing Alec Gilroy short shrift when he asked her to add extra salt to make the customers thirsty so they'd drink more, and was livid when new barmaid Shelley Unwin dared to add some extra herbs. Fred Elliott plotted to steal the recipe, but she was soon wise to his scam. To get her own back she gave him the ingredients list including an extra eye-popping amount of pepper; the first customer to taste it, Norris Cole, threatened to sue.

She may have passed away but her hotpot legacy lives on and Sean Tully was shocked to be handed a letter at her wake bequeathing him the full recipe. However, the dish's future at the Rovers was thrown into doubt

'You've not served food till you've brandished Betty's hotpot.'

Fred to new barmaid Michelle

▲ Sean keeps Betty's secret recipe close to his chest.
▶ Betty gets to grips with her hotpot.
▶ Fred nabs the recipe.

when Stella Price insisted an exhausted Sean come over during his lunch breaks from the factory and make some more. Unable to keep up with the demand, he resigned from his job at the Rovers, taking Betty's recipe with him.

Spotting an opportunity to lure punters away from the Rovers, Nick Tilsley hired Sean to serve the dish at the bistro instead. Furious, Stella threatened legal action insisting the Rovers owned the intellectual property rights to the recipe and Rita Sullivan informed a conscience-stricken Sean that Betty would be turning in her grave if she knew hotpot was no longer on the Rovers' menu.

When the bistro's oven broke, Stella agreed to let Sean cook the hotpot at the pub for the street's jubilee party. But she then refused to let him serve it, announcing she'd taken out an injunction on it, making it her property. Nick played along, until Sean realised he'd been set up and everyone agreed that Betty's dish should go back to the Rovers where it belonged and all hotpot hostilities were ended.

'How beautiful is that ... if you opened me up you'd find half-man, half-hotpot.'

Jack tucks in

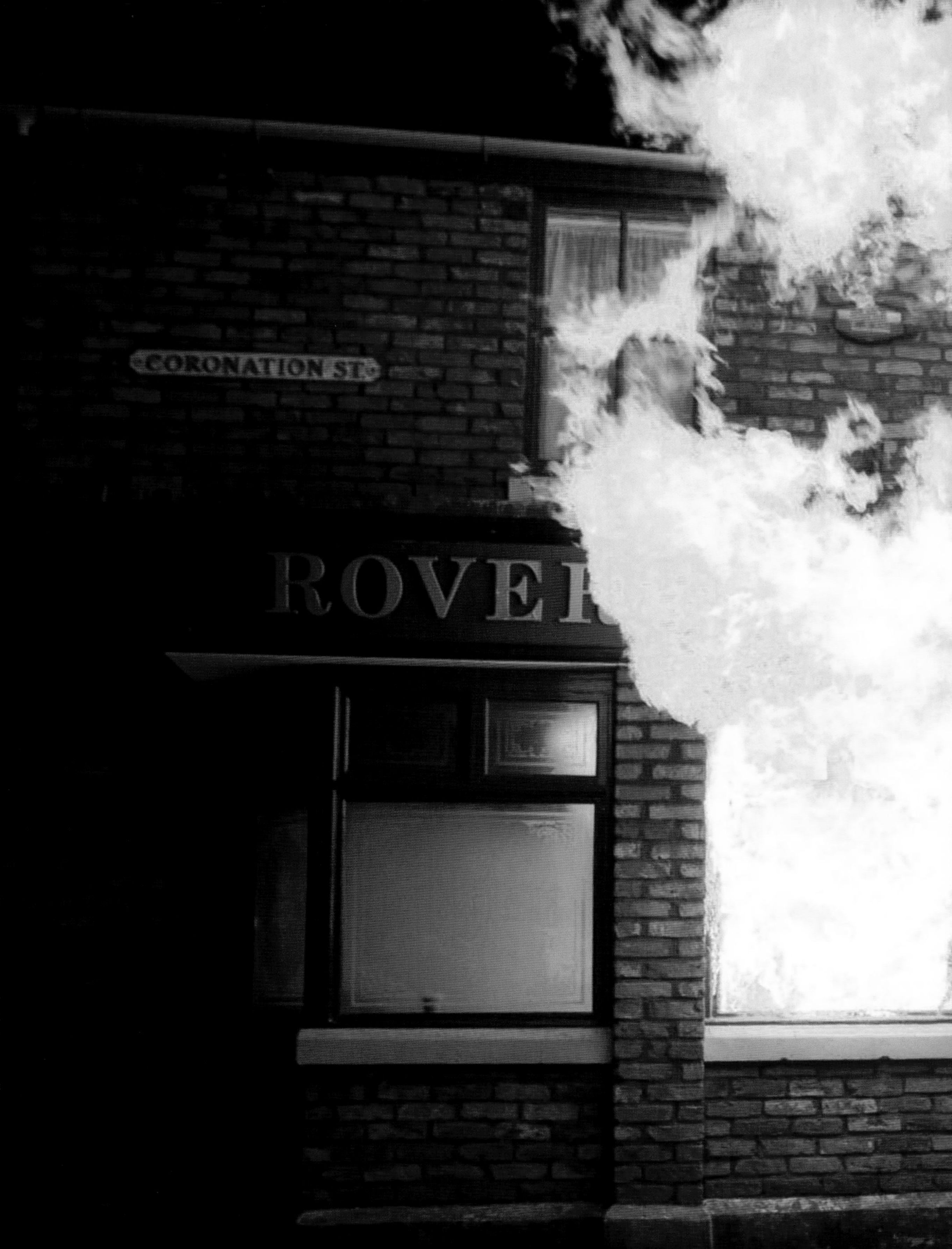
CORONATION ST.
ROVER

Trouble at the Rovers

It's in times of trouble that the Rovers comes into its own as a hub where the community can pull together. But when the pub itself is in dire straits the regulars are reminded just how much their beloved local means to them. From the disastrous lorry crash in 1979 where baby Tracy narrowly escaped death, to the catastrophic fires that devastated the pub in both 1986 and 2013, the Rovers Return has often faced an uncertain future...

The Lorry Crash

7 March 1979

'Why all this senseless, stupid destruction of life and property? What is the point of beginning anything, anything at all, if eventually you are going to destroy it?'

Annie

Deirdre Langton had only popped into the Rovers to look at a knitting pattern from Annie Walker, but very quickly she found herself facing every mother's nightmare – a terrifying turn of events that still haunts her to this day. Knowing that Annie didn't approve of the presence of children on her licensed premises, Deirdre – who had recently split with husband Ray – left her two-year-old daughter Tracy outside the pub in her pushchair while she hurried inside.

Deirdre and Annie had only been in the back room for a matter of minutes when they were interrupted by a deafening crash that seemed to shake the Rovers to its very core. While Annie froze, Deirdre's first thought was for toddler Tracy and she sped back through the bar where, amongst the shattered glass and falling beams, barmaids Betty Turpin and Bet Lynch were helping each other up having been thrown to the ground by the blast. The lunchtime regulars were also sprawled across the floor, but in a blind panic Deirdre stumbled past them and wrenched open the pub doors. Where only moments before she'd left Tracy in her pram, there now stood a huge mountain of timber from an enormous overturned lorry that had crashed into the pub.

As the local residents and the machinists from Baldwin's Casuals rushed out into the street on hearing the smash, they watched helplessly as Deirdre scrabbled frantically through the timber, screaming Tracy's name. Neighbour Ken Barlow instructed Rita Fairclough to call the police and a thankful Hilda Ogden muttered

▶ Tracy is nowhere to be seen as Deirdre searches for her daughter.

to herself with relief that for once her other half Stan wasn't inside – he'd gone to have his hair cut.

It was then that Bet heard Deirdre's screams and sent Betty outside to find out what was going on. The barmaid tried to calm her down but to no avail, as the panic-stricken young mum continued to pull at the timber screaming, 'Tracy's here! I left Tracy here!'

Inside, where moments before they'd been enjoying a lunchtime pint, shop-keeper Alf Roberts now lay unconscious under the rubble and factory owner Mike Baldwin was in pain on the floor, his suit ripped and torn and his leg trapped under the debris. Fortunately for Len Fairclough,

▲ Hilda, Vera and Ena watch the drama unfold.
▶ Distraught Deirdre is helped to safety.

he had escaped with a few cuts and a shoulder injury. Annie, however, had frozen in shock and continued to stare into the middle distance as chaos ensued around her. As she attempted to snap out of it she spotted Alf on the floor, her hand flew to her mouth and she started to garble. 'Poor Alf, he's dead isn't he? He looks dead!' Bet intervened and tried to soothe her. 'Now Mrs Walker, Alf's not dead, nobody's dead.' On hearing the fire engine sirens Bet added softly: 'There's someone here to help us now so you come and sit down,' and led a trembling Annie into the back room.

Bet then tended to Mike who complained when she offered him a glass of water as opposed to his usual whisky. 'It's my flamin' leg that's injured, not me throat,' he quipped, clearly in pain. Meanwhile a concerned Len stayed by his friend Alf's side. 'It's all right mate, we'll have you out of here in no time, no danger,' he soothed.

Back outside the police and the fire services, along with Ken, climbed up on top of the rubble and tried to calm Deirdre down as she crawled over the fallen wood and attempted to dig for her baby. 'You'll do no good doing that, love, in fact you might make things worse,' asserted a policeman as he and Ken removed her from the rubble. Family friend Emily Bishop escorted her into Number 3 and offered Deirdre a sugary cup of tea in an effort to get

her to compose herself. But Deirdre insisted Tracy needed her and attempted to leave, only to be stopped in her tracks by the plain-speaking Ena Sharples, who managed to talk some sense into her. 'Of course Tracy wants you, but they have to find her first. And they are looking hard, very hard. Now sit yerself down and we'll come and tell you when she's found – and she's going to be found, make no mistake about that.' An exhausted Deirdre sank back into a chair, still distraught. 'But I only left her for a minute and it wasn't even a minute...' she babbled.

A policeman called for backup and issued orders. 'Don't let anybody go near. And put Control in the picture. Tell 'em we need more bodies. It's a major incident.' As more members of the emergency services arrived they were briefed on the state of play. 'All the mother said was that she left the baby outside in her pushchair then next thing ... wallop,' a senior officer explained. The fire brigade called for silence from the gathered throng as they attempted to listen for any sign of life from Tracy under the dangerously unstable rubble. But there was no sound. The police braced themselves as they prepared to tell Deirdre her little girl was probably dead.

Alf was taken to hospital in an ambulance, but while he was still breathing he showed worryingly little other sign of life. The driver of the lorry was found dead – it turned out he'd had a heart attack at the wheel, which had caused the accident. Blaming herself, Deirdre was convinced Tracy was also dead and rolled onto her side, sobbing hysterically into Emily's sofa. 'It's all my fault. First there were me and Ray and I sent him away. Now she's gone and it's all

'Families have to stick together. That's what you have a family for. They're like flowers. Take one petal away and before you know it, it's all gone. Tracy's dead like me and Ray. Her family's dead so she's dead. It follows. Logical.'

Deirdre fears the worst

my fault. I started it. Families have to stick together. That's what you have a family for. They're like flowers. Take one petal away and before you know it, it's all gone. Tracy's dead like me and Ray. Her family's dead so she's dead. It follows. Logical. How am I going to tell Ray? He adored her...' At the table a sombre Ena said a special prayer for the safe return of Tracy.

In the back room of the Rovers Annie clamped her hands to her ears to block out the sounds of sirens. Betty attempted to bring her out of herself by offering her tea, but the landlady had more profound matters on her mind. 'The gates of hell will sound like that when they swing open to receive us all,' she declared. 'Has the world gone mad? Why do these things happen? What's the point? Why all this senseless stupid destruction of life and property? What is the point of beginning anything, anything at all, if eventually you are going to destroy it?'

Meanwhile, in the bar, having supported everyone else and seen the last of the injured regulars off the premises, the shock of it all finally hit Bet. She broke down to Rita Fairclough at the thought of Tracy trapped under the rubble. Rita reassured her pal and led her behind the bar for a much-needed slug of brandy.

On the doorstep of Number 3 a policeman explained to Emily that after a thorough search they'd found Tracy's doll under the rubble but there was no sign of Tracy herself. This was a good thing as it meant she couldn't have been there when the lorry crashed. Her face lighting up at the news, Emily dashed into the parlour to tell Deirdre her daughter was likely to be alive, but the back door

◄ Onlookers Rita and Hilda inform Renee that Alf is injured.

was wide open and the grieving mum was nowhere to be seen. When CID arrived on the scene, they asked whether Deirdre was unstable and could have killed Tracy herself.

At the hospital, Mike had broken ribs, slight concussion and a fractured ankle, Len had a head cut and sprained shoulder and Betty was treated for cuts. In his hospital bed Alf was still unconscious, and his distressed wife Renee was informed he'd fractured his skull and would need a brain scan.

At the same time an inconsolable Deirdre walked the streets in a haze of tears and grief, convinced Tracy had been crushed to death. She stopped on a canal bridge and stared over the edge as if to contemplate suicide. Back at Number 3 Emily suddenly recalled a young mentally unstable girl called Sally Norton who Deirdre had befriended in the maternity hospital. She'd been forced to give up her own baby for adoption and was now back on the scene.

Emily gave Sally's description to the police and sure enough they found her playing mum with Tracy in a park – she'd snatched her from her pram moments before the lorry had crashed. Unharmed, Tracy was swiftly returned to Emily, who drove around the area with Len in his van searching for Deirdre. They found her dazed and confused on the canal side, refusing to believe Tracy was alive. But when she saw her little girl's smiling face, Deirdre's trance was broken and there were tears of joy as mother and daughter were reunited. When she recovered from the trauma of the day, Deirdre admitted she'd always feel grateful to Sally Norton for effectively saving her daughter's life.

Back on the street Len and Eddie Yeats boarded up the broken pub windows, but when Mr Cresswell from the brewery didn't immediately return Annie's calls she became convinced Newton & Ridley were preparing to tell her they'd rather pull the pub down than pay for repairs. But after a phone call that evening Annie made an announcement. 'Well, I do have some good news amid the gloom! I am very relieved to be able to tell you the future of the Rovers has never been in any doubt!' The pub was safe, Alf was soon out of his coma and back supping his pint at the bar and it was business as usual at the Rovers Return.

'I'm sorry, Rita, I hardly ever cry, you know. I can't afford to, not when I've got this much eye-liner and mascara on.'

Bet

Pub on Fire

18 June 1986

'I bet you any money she's been smoking in bed.'

Vera

Little did landlady Bet Lynch know that when she allowed pot-man Jack Duckworth to tinker with the Rovers' fuse box it would result in her fighting for her life – and her livelihood. All day the beer pumps and the bar lights had been flickering on and off, and despite the fact he had absolutely zero experience when it came to electrics, Bet put her faith in Jack's DIY skills. 'Worry not, booze artists. Cometh the hour, cometh the man and the knowledge. Super-spark will soon have the ale flowing,' she reassured the regulars. To keep everyone entertained as the night drew in, she arranged for a local musician to play and everyone settled in for a good old-fashioned singsong around the piano by candlelight.

It was almost an anti-climax when Jack got the lights working again by substituting a much heftier fuse for the smaller ones that had kept on blowing. He enjoyed his moment in the limelight and Bet was delighted, declaring the evening a great success. Leaving

◀ Bet and Jack prepare to pull pints by torchlight.
▶ The first sign of fire as smoke seeps from the Rovers' doors.

the clearing up until morning, she headed up to bed with a trashy novel.

But while Bet slept soundly, the overheated fuse box began to spark and fizz, and soon all of the cellar was ablaze. It was loved-up young mechanic Kevin Webster and his girlfriend Sally Seddon who first noticed something was wrong. At 5.30am, just as the milkman was doing his early morning round, they'd been dropped back in Weatherfield after an all-nighter in Sheffield and were giggling away. Just as Kevin moved in for a kiss he didn't see passion in Sally's face but fear. 'Kevin...' she gasped. 'Fire!'

Kevin turned to look and they both gazed at the smoke seeping out from under the Rovers' doors. Kevin ran straight over to the pub and tried to get inside, with Sally screaming at him not to do anything stupid. He immediately took control of the situation. 'Quick, go to the Barlows'. Tell them to phone the brigade, wake them up!' he yelled at her. He then started to bang furiously on the Rovers' doors and bellowed for Bet to get up. But as he stood back and looked up at her bedroom window there was no sign of life as the curtains stayed firmly closed.

Alerted by all the commotion, caretaker Percy Sugden was quickly on the scene in his dressing gown, and instructed Kevin to come with him to the community centre where there was a ladder that could be used to reach up to Bet's bedroom.

Sally made her way down the street, banging on doors and shrieking at everyone to get out of their houses in case the fire spread. Ken, in his pyjamas, yelled to his wife as he took in the scene – 'Deirdre, get Tracy out!' – and then moved his car to make way for the fire brigade. When Kevin and Percy reappeared with the ladder, a shirtless Terry Duckworth also arrived and threw himself into action whilst neighbours Emily Bishop and Ivy Tilsley watched on agog.

On hearing the commotion outside her window Bet had finally woken but was blinded by smoke. Whimpering with fear and trying to catch her breath, she managed to feel her way to the top of the stairs but her path was blocked by the now-roaring flames. Realising she was trapped, she let out a piercing scream, before fumbling her way back into the bedroom, coughing violently as she slammed the door behind her. Sobbing and choking at the same time, she slid down behind the bedroom door before falling to her knees and vomiting. In one final attempt to escape the smoke and save her life, she slowly and painfully dragged herself to the window, but just as she thought she'd made it she collapsed unconscious from the noxious fumes while the fire raged around her.

Sitting inside their car as Jack attempted to move it, Vera was convinced she knew how the fire had started. 'I bet you any money she's been smoking in bed,' she sniffed. Jack winced and looked decidedly shifty; he had a very strong feeling that he'd caused the fire by putting in the wrong fuse.

While Kevin scurried up the ladder the residents shouted suggestions as to what was the best way to get in, and Terry handed him a brick which he used to smash through the window. But just as Kevin reached inside the smoke-filled room, there was a huge explosion downstairs, the windows shattered and the ferocious flames continued to ravage the building. Terrified for Kevin's safety, Sally couldn't look and was comforted by Emily.

▼ The residents join forces to save Bet.
▶ As the fire spreads the emergency services come to Bet's rescue.

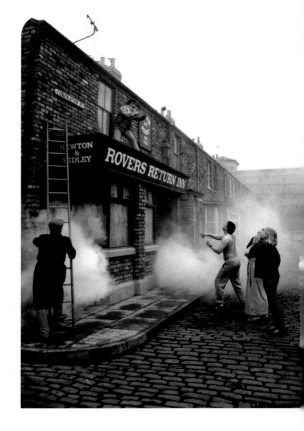

To everyone's relief the fire brigade arrived in the nick of time. 'Who's up there?' a foreman asked Terry. 'My mate,' he replied, fearing the worst. 'And the woman who runs the pub, Bet Lynch.'

Inside the firemen found a spluttering Kevin trying to drag Bet's seemingly lifeless body to safety. Letting the professionals take over, Kevin headed back down the ladder to cheers from the residents while both Sally and his landlady Hilda Ogden fussed over their hero. 'What's wrong with you?' asked Vera, as a worried Jack remained tense and solemn. 'Frightened of crackin' your face?'

But Jack was secretly praying he wasn't the cause of this dreadful catastrophe.

In her smoke-singed white nightdress Bet's limp body was carried down the ladder and carefully positioned onto a stretcher. The residents gathered round as an oxygen mask was placed over her face. But it was only in the back of the ambulance, as the vehicle sped on its way to Weatherfield General, that Bet flickered back into life. 'Could you hang on a bit, love, and let me get me face on?' she joked feebly.

◄ A burnt-out shell; the pub is devastated by the fire.
► Hilda is the guest of honour as the Rovers reopens.

The firemen did what they could to rescue the pub but by the time they'd put out the last of the flames the building was nothing but a burnt-out shell. However, the officials had no trouble finding out what had caused the fire – it was the faulty electrics.

Back on the street, after Ken and Deirdre had given her a lift to visit Bet in hospital, barmaid Betty approached a fireman clearing up outside. 'Are those her things?' she asked, pointing to a small charred pile of Bet's belongings. 'Yes they are. Who are you?' 'Well, I'm Betty Turpin, I work there...' she paused and then, shaking her head in dismay as she surveyed the blackened wreckage, added, 'Well, I did.'

Looking inside, Betty gasped as she took in the destruction the fire had caused. It was a scorched shell, with no remnants of the bright, busy and bustling pub it had once been. 'Well, that's what fire does,' remarked a policeman. 'I think you were lucky, Mr Barlow,' he added, turning to Ken. The Rovers next-door neighbour pulled Deirdre close to him, and the Barlows stood in shocked silence as they dwelt on the horror of what could've been.

Later that day, a guilt-ridden and anxious Jack met up with Betty and fellow barmaid Gloria Todd, who'd just got back from a meeting at the brewery. It wasn't good news and Jack's torment increased as Betty explained. 'He was one of the Ridleys and he said they'd had an emergency meeting and they'd

'I've pinned up a little card next to the phone. Number on it's an electrician. If a fuse ever blows, that's who you ring. We've got this place back – let's try and hang on to it, eh?'
Bet to Jack

been round to the Rovers and inspected it and it'd be cheaper to pull it down.'

The following day Bet discharged herself from hospital and, with nowhere else to go, she moved in with Betty. She visited the gutted pub and after seeing the bare, boarded-up remains of her now-wrecked Rovers, she broke down to good pal Rita. Not knowing what the future held, she told Rita she'd had enough of picking herself up off the floor.

Later she met with the brewery bosses and despite the fact she'd by now worked out that Jack's bodged attempt at fixing the electrics had caused the blaze, Bet insisted on taking the blame for the fire by admitting she should have used a qualified electrician. She was stunned and relieved when George Newton revealed the brewery was aware the wiring had needed updating and they'd had a change of heart over the pub's future. Instead of demolishing the premises, they were now planning a complete renovation!

Two months later the Rovers had its grand reopening and long-serving employee Hilda was the guest of honour and got to cut the ribbon. After he came crawling, Bet even gave Jack his job back, but on one very strict condition: 'I've pinned up a little card next to the phone,' she said firmly. 'Number on it's an electrician. If a fuse ever blows, that's who you ring. We've got this place back – let's try and hang on to it, eh?'

The Rovers Re-burns

18 March 2013

'Breaks my heart, you know, looking at the pub like that. All that time, work and effort just gone up in smoke in a couple of minutes.'

Stella

After another run-in with her increasingly creepy ex, Karl Munro, Rovers' landlady Stella Price was ready to try and let her hair down. Along with her mum Gloria and daughter Eva, she headed over to the bistro to see some of the male regulars strip 'Full Monty'-style for charity. But stepping into a fun night out, she also walked straight into a confrontation with a sozzled Sunita Alahan. Ever since Stella discovered Karl had been cheating on her with her former friend there'd been no love lost between the two women, so when Stella – who was now dating toyboy builder Jason Grimshaw – heard that Dev and Sunita were giving their relationship another go, she warned Dev against giving his adulterous ex a second chance. Dev took on board what Stella was telling him and ended it for good with a devastated Sunita.

In the bistro Sunita gave the interfering landlady a piece of her mind before chucking her drink all over her. No longer in the party mood, Stella headed home for some peace and quiet and a relaxing bath. But Stella wasn't alone in the Rovers and as she enjoyed her

▼ ▶ Sunita lays into Stella, before being abandoned in the burning cellar by arsonist Karl.

180

hot soak, a fire was taking hold down in the cellar, started by none other than her twisted ex, Karl, who had no idea his precious Stella had returned home unexpectedly.

Meanwhile Sunita had followed Karl into the Rovers after spying him sneaking down the back alleyway and caught him in the act. 'What the hell are you doing?' she gasped, as she tried to take in what she had stumbled upon.

'It's the only way,' replied the twisted fire-starter. 'You know as much as anyone that I'm meant to be with Stella and that means getting rid of Jason. She loves this place. If she thinks Jason's botched the electrics and caused the fire … he's finished. Then me and Stella will pick up where we left off.'

'You really believe that, don't you? You're mad!' she gulped. Realising Karl had finally lost the plot, Sunita tried to escape but he grabbed her, determined his warped plan wasn't going to fail. 'You're not gonna ruin things for me again!' he snarled as they grappled, but as Sunita struggled to break free she stumbled backwards and fell down the cellar steps, her head hitting a barrel before she landed with a sickening thud. In a blind panic, thinking he'd killed Sunita, Karl fled and left her motionless, surrounded by flickering flames. He returned to the bistro just in time to join the stripping finale with the rest of the boys, who'd been oblivious to his absence.

In the end it was Norris Cole who raised the alarm after he and Emily Bishop spotted smoke billowing out from under the pub's doors. As the Full Monty reached its climax and the lads were about to reveal all, Norris rushed in and alerted everyone that the pub was on fire. Gloria, Eva and Leanne became hysterical as it dawned on them Stella was probably inside the burning building.

Back at the pub, Stella was choking for breath as smoke filled the bathroom. Realising she had to escape quickly, she grabbed a towel and pulled it to her face before heading out onto the landing. However, here the smoke was even thicker than before and, blinded by the acrid fumes and scorching flames, she got down on all fours and crawled, spluttering, back towards the bedroom.

As the locals headed out into the street to see what was happening, Karl mingled with the crowd but was horrified to spot a screaming Stella at the bedroom window trying to smash the glass with a table lamp. Off-duty fireman Paul Kershaw held Jason back. 'Until the fire crews arrive, I'm in charge. No one goes in that building,' he ordered. Meanwhile Karl had snuck round the back and had let himself in with his stolen set of keys, storming into the flames to save Stella with his coat over his head. But just as he reached his ex the burning stairs suddenly collapsed into the fiery abyss – trapped, they stared at each other, both rigid with fear.

◀ Stella screams for help.
▶ The shocked residents react as the fire takes hold.

In the chaos, Dev and the rest of the neighbours had no idea Sunita was inside the pub. Down in the cellar she'd regained consciousness and was trying to escape, navigating her way through a wall of fire in the main bar area. But before she could get to the window and signal for help, she was overpowered by smoke and collapsed in the back room.

As the flames thickened, the crowd outside were shocked to see Karl's face at the bedroom window as well as Stella's. Losing consciousness, Stella crumpled onto the floor and Karl lay protectively next to her, offering scant comfort. 'At least we'll die together. I love you.'

Unable to stand back and watch any longer, Jason fetched ladders from the builders' yard, but in the end it was Paul's colleague Toni Griffiths who insisted on entering the burning pub, despite his girlfriend Eileen Grimshaw's pleas that they wait for the emergency services. Minutes later the fire brigade arrived and rescued Stella and Sunita, who were both alive but badly injured. Toni pulled Karl

out of the building, but as he was carried to safety, part of the interior structure collapsed, swallowing up Toni in the process. When Stella went into respiratory arrest in the back of the ambulance, Gloria held her daughter's hand and muttered a silent prayer.

But there was terrible news for Paul. After fellow fire officers made a search of the Rovers, they approached their colleague and he turned in shock to the onlookers. 'She's dead, Toni, she's dead,' he said in disbelief. Traumatised by her death, he later agonised 'Why the hell didn't I stop her?'

At the hospital Dev kept vigil by Sunita's bedside where she was on a life-support machine, repeatedly telling her how much he loved her and begging her to wake up. Meanwhile an emotional Gloria pleaded with her daughter to survive. 'Are you listening to your mother? I'm the flaky one in this relationship. I've left you so many times. Do you remember when I told you I was going to Spain? Emigrating, I said. You were over by the the hob cooking Eva's tea. I can see you now. "Emigrating!" You took it all in your stride. Didn't blink an eyelid. I've always envied you, so rooted and strong. Sometimes I think I've only done one thing properly, one thing right, in the whole of my life. And that's you. Mothers go first. That's the deal. Don't leave me, sweetheart,' she sobbed as she clutched her daughter's hand.

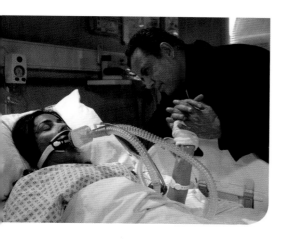

Much to her family's relief, Stella regained consciousness, although boyfriend Jason was crushed when the first word out of her mouth was the name of her supposed saviour, Karl. Back on the street, talk turned to what or who may have started the fire and when early investigations pointed to Jason's work on the electrics being the cause, the beleaguered builder tried to defend himself. Knowing he had done everything by the book and convinced that Karl had started the fire, Jason voiced his suspicions, but no one believed Karl was anything other than the hero of the hour.

Luckily for Jason, the police found evidence the fire had been started deliberately, and Gloria made it clear that, in her opinion, there was only one possible culprit – the scorned, spurned and angry Sunita.

Karl could scarcely believe his luck – Sunita was in the frame for the tragedy and he stopped at nothing to ensure she was going to take the blame. He sneaked into her hospital room as she fought for her life and placed her limp hand over the stolen set of Rovers' keys to cover them with her fingerprints. He then carefully switched them with the house keys from the bedside cabinet that held the rest of her personal effects. When the police discovered the keys, it was further confirmation Sunita had to be the arsonist, much to the shock and disbelief of Dev and Stella.

> *'Mothers go first. That's the deal. Don't leave me, sweetheart.'*
> **Gloria to Stella**

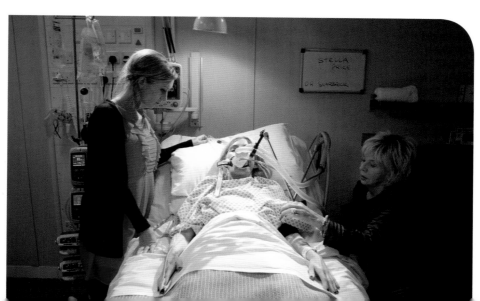

When Stella was discharged from hospital, it was Karl who made sure he was by her side to comfort her when she saw the burnt-out pub for the first time. She then agreed he could move into their temporary accommodation at Number 13 until he sorted himself out, despite Jason's protestations. One night, snuggled up on the sofa together, Stella apologised to Karl for misjudging him and it looked like Karl's plan was working a treat when the pair kissed.

However, he hadn't accounted for Sunita's recovery, and there was a glimmer of hope when her eyes began to flicker. Convinced of Sunita's innocence, an overjoyed Dev now knew it was just a matter of time before she was able to talk and tell them the truth about the fire. A panicked Karl also knew she was the one person who could expose his wicked deed, so he took drastic action by sneaking into her hospital room and killing her.

When Stella and Karl revealed they were back together, Gloria and Eva were thrilled, whereas daughter Leanne remained convinced that a leopard never changes his spots. She grew increasingly suspicious when she saw how quickly Karl wanted to get married and how much pressure he was putting Stella under.

Later, a menacing Karl showed his true colours when he confronted and threatened Leanne. But when she voiced her concerns to Stella, her mum had other things on her mind – the insurance company had refused to pay out for the Rovers' fire, the bank had turned down her loan application and she faced financial ruin. Leanne offered to invest the money she got from the bookies into the Rovers on one condition – her mother had to stop seeing Karl. Stella refused to be blackmailed and informed Leanne that she and Karl had got engaged.

▼ Owen rebuilds the Rovers for Stella.
▶ Champagne all round at the grand reopening.

Worried Leanne insisted she was making a huge mistake but when a down-on-her-luck Stella started work at the Bistro as a cleaner, with Gail as her supervisor, Leanne began to feel sorry for her mum.

Eventually, after two months of refurbishment, the Rovers was ready to open its doors again, funded largely by Gloria, who had secretly inherited a wad of cash from her late fiancé Eric's will after all. Leanne had had a

Norris: *'They've not exactly overhauled it, have they?'*
Audrey: *'Good. I hate them glass and chrome places. Everywhere you look there's you looking back.'*

change of heart and had stumped up £10,000 towards the fixtures and fittings.

Out of respect for those who'd died, Stella wanted a low-key reopening of the pub, but Gloria was determined to party, dressed up to the nines (having already changed her outfit twice), she started ringing a bell as the queuing regulars bustled in. 'Welcome! The Rovers is returned – to you!' she trilled. 'Grab some fizz!' The general consensus was that the new-look pub had retained its comforting charm and Rita brought along a freshly-framed picture of veteran barmaid Betty Williams for the wall, to replace the one destroyed in the fire.

Dev plucked up the courage to attend in Sunita's memory, but became tearful. 'Poor thing,' sighed Leanne, as he hurried out. 'Must be like visiting her grave coming in here.' Looking around at the packed bar it was an emotional night for everyone and Stella – egged on by Gloria – made a hesitant but heartfelt speech which summed up the mood. 'My grandma used to say buildings stored memories in bricks and mortar. I reckon this pub's got lots of those already, but now it has got a few more that we'll never forget. So raise a glass with me – to present and absent friends!'

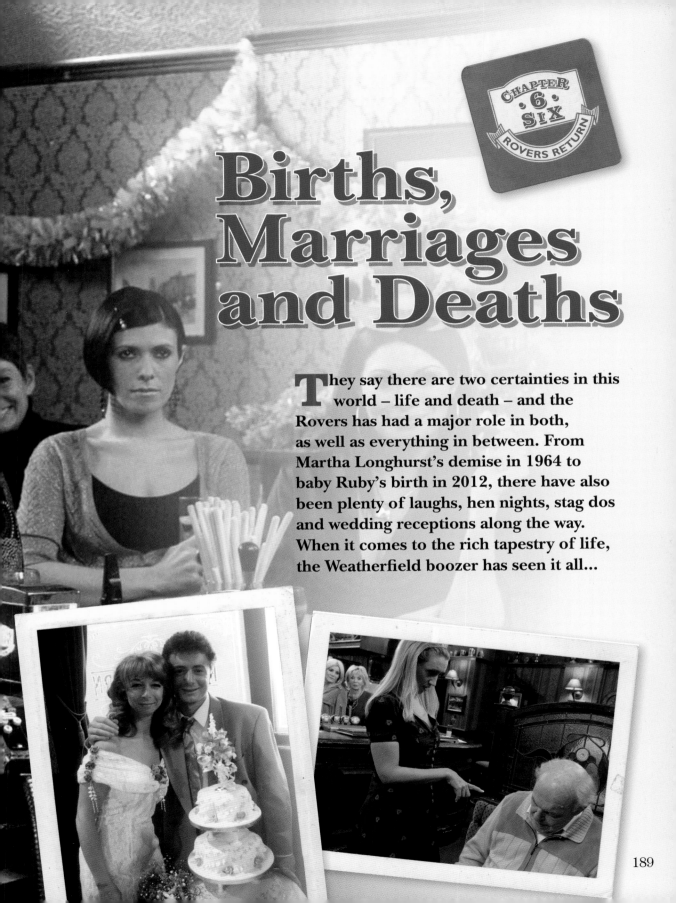

Births, Marriages and Deaths

They say there are two certainties in this world – life and death – and the Rovers has had a major role in both, as well as everything in between. From Martha Longhurst's demise in 1964 to baby Ruby's birth in 2012, there have also been plenty of laughs, hen nights, stag dos and wedding receptions along the way. When it comes to the rich tapestry of life, the Weatherfield boozer has seen it all...

Births

Christopher Hewitt
4 August 1962

While husband Harry was enjoying himself at Ken and Valerie Barlow's wedding, former barmaid Concepta Hewitt was making landlord Jack a brew at the Rovers. She also happened to be heavily pregnant, and instead of just giving Jack his cup of tea, she also gave him a huge shock by going into labour. He hurried her to hospital and a few days later she gave birth to baby Christopher, who weighed 7lb 3oz.

'Looks like your living room's not going to be turned into a maternity ward after all, Mrs Walker!'

Audrey to a relieved Annie

Nick Tilsley
31 December 1980

Gail Tilsley's contractions began during the Rovers' New Year's Eve celebrations, and after being fussed over in the back room by dad-to-be Brian and their mothers, Audrey and Ivy, she was led panting through the bar to the ambulance outside. A nervous Audrey waited in the pub until she got a phone call from Brian just before midnight, with the news she'd been waiting for. 'It's a boy!' she announced to cheers. 'He weighs 7lb 2oz and mother and son are doing very well!'

Brad Armstrong
14 February 1997

Tricia Armstrong was five weeks away from her due date and was helping out behind the bar on Valentine's Day when she went into sudden early labour with Terry Duckworth's son. Landlord grandparents Jack and Vera were out at a brewery dance, so it was up to senior barmaid Betty – with a helping hand from Tricia's son Jamie – to deliver baby Brad in the back room.

Dylan Wilson
22 February 2008

It was all hands on deck when Violet Wilson went into labour, but luckily Marcus Dent, a sonographer at Weatherfield General, was there to take control of proceedings. He propped up the barmaid in a booth and instructed a green-looking Vernon Tomlin to bring towels. 'Anything I can get you, Vi?' asked her sister Lauren. 'I suppose a double vodka's out of the question...?' gasped the barmaid, between huffs and puffs. After one final agonising push, baby Dylan was born, and sperm-donor and Violet's gay best friend Sean was overwhelmed. 'I swear he turned and looked straight at me ... I was the first face he saw,' he spluttered, gazing tearily at his son. But Sean's happiness was short-lived when Violet, feeling smothered by him, put her boyfriend Jamie Baldwin's name on the birth certificate and did a runner to London.

'You should have heard what came out of my mouth when I gave birth – you could hear me in Cheshire.'

Eileen comforts Violet

191

Ruby Soames
9 September 2012

Former copper and full-time tormentor Kirsty Soames was having a sly and vicious row with arch-enemy Tina McIntyre. The barmaid finally snapped and shoved the heavily-pregnant Kirsty, who went crashing into a bar stool. Kirsty's waters broke and, with no time to get to hospital, she gave birth in the back room aided by Marcus (now a midwife) while being fussed over by landlady Stella's mother, Gloria Price. Fiancé Tyrone Dobbs arrived just in time to see his adored daughter Ruby enter the world.

'When I was at school I was the kid with the dirty neck who whiffed a bit. Not you. You're gonna have a clean uniform every day. Ribbons in your hair. And if you don't play Mary in the Nativity, Brian Packham's gonna get a potato up his exhaust pipe.'

Tyrone to newborn Ruby

Jake Windass
26 May 2013

Surrogate mum Tina was utterly worn out by recent events, which included the strain of being entangled in the lives of overbearing biological parents Izzy Armstrong and Gary Windass, and having experienced Gary making a drunken pass at her. In the middle of the pub's reopening bash, which she'd helped to organise, she realised she was having contractions — eight weeks early! An ambulance was swiftly called and the barmaid gave birth at Weatherfield General to a boy named Jake.

'Trust Tina to upstage me. Hardly a party mood now, is it?'

Gloria

Will You Marry Me?

The roll call of Rovers proposals...

Betty Turpin & Bet Lynch & Fred Gee, 1978

Pot-man Fred was desperate to get his own pub from the brewery, but was told he'd need to be married to improve his chances. Fred didn't cast his net very wide and first asked Betty, who turned him down flat. Later, over tea in the back room, while nervously chomping on a sandwich Fred spluttered out a proposal to a mortified Bet. She let him down gently, explaining she could only marry for love.

Tina Fowler & Eddie Ramsden, 1990

Tina's builder boyfriend Eddie, who was locked in a custody battle with the mother of his child, told her he'd stand a better chance in court if he were married. The loved-up barmaid agreed to be his wife, but on her hen night Eddie announced he was reuniting with his ex. After sobbing her heart out, Tina bounced back and cut her wedding cake in the Rovers anyway!

Phyllis Pearce & Percy Sugden, 1996

Using the opportunity of a leap year, blue-rinsed pensioner Phyllis Pearce proposed to the longstanding man of her dreams, Percy Sugden. However, she was unaware that rival-in-love Maud Grimes had also popped the question. Convinced the pair were taking the mickey out of him, pursed-lipped Percy turned them both down.

Maureen Holdsworth & Fred Elliott, 1997

Fred's first bungled attempt to persuade corner-shop owner Maureen to marry him took place in the Rovers when he suddenly blurted out: 'I want to marry you!' Although she enjoyed his company, she was convinced he just wanted to get his hands on her premises, so she turned him down. A determined and besotted Fred proposed twice more before she finally agreed.

Natalie Horrocks & Kevin Webster, 1998

Kevin resented Natalie's imminent nuptials to Des Barnes and hung around the engagement party getting drunk and being miserable. He laid into his ex, insisting she was making a huge mistake and should marry him instead. An angry Natalie declined and Alec threw him out.

Sally Webster & Danny Hargreaves, 2000

Former market-stall holder Danny proposed on New Year's Eve in the midst of Natalie's leaving do. He wanted Sally to move away from Weatherfield and from Kevin but she refused because of their girls. On the morning of their wedding a few months later, Sally confessed to a one-night stand with Kevin, and heartbroken Danny called off the ceremony and left town.

Karen Phillips & Steve McDonald, 2001

When Janice Battersby bet Karen two days' wages that she couldn't get cabbie boss Steve down the aisle, Karen was up for the challenge. Janice was gobsmacked when Steve (who was now in on the joke) turned up in the Rovers with a bunch of flowers and got down on one knee. After being dared to marry for a bet and both refusing to back down, the pair genuinely fell for each other.

Shelley Unwin & Peter Barlow, 2002

Shelley was delighted when, out of the blue, bookie Peter proposed to her in the back room. They married the following year, but when a stranger called Lucy showed up at the pub with a wedding album to show her, she realised Peter had another blushing bride in his life. Worse still, Lucy went on to reveal she and Peter had a baby boy called Simon. Both women agreed to get revenge on the two-timing bigamist by reporting him to the police. Shelley then introduced Lucy and secret son Simon to everyone in the bar. The punters looked on aghast at the revelations, including mortified in-laws Ken and Deirdre who'd also been kept in the dark about Peter's double-wedded bliss *and* their grandson.

Fiz Brown & Tyrone Dobbs, 2004

Tyrone was competing with Kirk for Fiz's hand, but after Kirk's grand gesture of serenading her in the street, Tyrone merely blurted out the question in the pub that lunchtime. Fiz let it be known she was unimpressed by his lack of imagination, so Tyrone upped his game and attempted to propose on horseback. But before he had the chance to pop the question, his pony sped away, causing him to fall off in Tile Street and he ended up with his arm in a sling.

Fiz Brown & Kirk Sutherland, 2004

Penniless Kirk stole a ring from a jeweller's and – too panicked to actually propose – slipped it into Fiz's drink. She choked on it, but saw the funny side and agreed to marry him.

Claire Casey & Ashley Peacock, 2004

Still in their decorating overalls, Ashley and former nanny Claire popped into the pub and when 'Stay' by Claire's favourite band, East 17, came on, the pair started to dance. Ashley then called for hush, dropped to one knee and declared his undying love for Claire.

'Every time I look at you I hear ... car horns beeping. Like after England have won a big game.'

Ashley to Claire

Bev Unwin & Fred Elliott, 2006

Even though Bev had already accepted Fred's unexpected proposal in a lay-by on a country road, an infatuated Fred wanted to do the job in the old-fashioned way. At their engagement party in the pub, he asked her to be his wife by getting down on one knee and presenting her with a ring.

Leanne Battersby & Danny Baldwin, 2006

Danny was trying to convince his son Jamie that his affair with Leanne wasn't just about lust, insisting he intended to marry her – at which point Leanne appeared and delightedly asked if he really meant it. Backed into a corner, Danny was forced to agree and Leanne gleefully accepted his 'proposal'. Eventually Danny dumped Leanne admitting he was still in love with his ex-wife Frankie.

Liz McDonald & Vernon Tomlin, 2007

Even though Liz was having an affair with Derek the drayman when Vernon proposed, the guilt-ridden landlady found herself saying yes. She instantly regretted it but a thrilled Vernon had already bounded into the bar to announce their engagement.

Doreen Fenwick & Norris Cole, 2007

Norris proposed to Rita's flirty friend Doreen, unaware that Ivor Priestley and George Trench had also done the same. Doreen insisted she needed time to carefully consider the proposals from her potential husbands, but an affronted Norris withdrew his offer.

Michelle Connor & Steve McDonald, 2008

Following his one-night stand with Becky, Michelle noticed Steve was behaving very oddly. His pal Lloyd tried to cover for him and insisted it was because Steve wanted to ask her to marry him. Steve felt forced to go through with the charade and a delighted Michelle accepted. However, just as Steve realised he really did love Michelle and wanted to be with her, Michelle found out he was just playing along with Lloyd's joke. So when he staged a more traditional proposal in the pub, Michelle let him have it with both barrels, then punched him and finished with him.

Steve: *'Michelle Connor, will you marry me?'*

Michelle: *'Not if you were the last flamin' fella on Earth!'*

Rita Sullivan & Colin Grimshaw, 2009

When Eileen's philandering dad Colin proposed to Rita during his 70th birthday party in the Rovers, she was thrilled, but her happiness didn't last long. Julie Carp's mother Paula arrived and revealed Colin had got her pregnant with Julie when she was just 14 years old. A shocked and disgusted Rita promptly told Colin she never wanted to see him again.

Becky Granger & Steve McDonald, 2009

When Becky told Steve she'd split up with Jason, he was delighted and got down on one knee to propose. She had no hesitation in saying yes and couldn't believe the rock of an engagement ring he placed on her finger. She also couldn't believe it when she later found out he'd recycled the ring originally meant for Michelle!

Leanne Battersby & Peter Barlow, 2010

Leanne suspected Peter of cheating on her with Michelle and confronted them in the pub during Ken and Deirdre's anniversary party. She was horrified to learn he had been planning a public proposal, and Michelle had been helping him select a ring. Leanne was gutted when Peter withdrew the offer, saying she clearly didn't trust him. The next day she surprised him in the pub and got down on one knee herself – much to her relief, he accepted.

Sunita Alahan & Dev Alahan, 2011

When her interfering aunties discovered Sunita and Dev were actually divorced, they focused on finding potential suitors for their niece. This prompted Dev to ask Sunita to marry him again but she refused, insisting they were fine as they were.

Carla Connor & Frank Foster, 2011

Sinister Frank had been planning a private proposal over dinner but when Carla proved awkward, he was forced to get down on one knee in the Rovers. Carla was mortified, told Frank he was embarrassing her and fled. Later she agreed to marry him, though, hoping to bury her feelings for Peter Barlow.

Tracy McDonald & Ryan Connor, 2012

Egged on by Steve, who was desperate to split them up, Ryan Connor asked his girlfriend Tracy to marry him, believing she was pregnant with his child. Steve's plan worked as Tracy had to admit there was no baby and Ryan realised she'd just been using him to get at Steve and his mum Michelle.

Leanne Barlow & Nick Tilsley, 2012

Nick was hurt when Leanne kept her divorce from Peter a secret. Encouraged by scheming Kylie Platt and his ex, Eva Price, Nick proposed to girlfriend Leanne in the Bistro, but she took offence at being rushed into marriage and refused. Realising she'd made a terrible mistake, Leanne turned the tables on Nick in the Rovers and begged him to marry her. He finally agreed, much to Eva's fury.

Eileen Grimshaw & Paul Kershaw, 2013

Jealous Eileen thought Paul had been cheating on her with his colleague, Toni, but in fact he'd been planning to propose. After much grovelling, Eileen met Paul in the Rovers where he accepted her apology. Then Paul got down on one knee to ask her to marry him.

Stags & Hens

Maxine Heavey & Ashley Peacock, 1999

Wanting to look her best on her wedding day, Maxine decided to opt out of a hen night and stay in with a face-pack, but Audrey and mum Doreen had other ideas. They blindfolded and handcuffed the young hairdresser and dragged her to the pub still wearing her pyjamas. Meanwhile Ashley's stag night at the golf club was proving to be a bit of a flop – they weren't allowed any music on the jukebox as there was a committee meeting taking place in the next room, Fred bored them all with stories about sausages, and the club steward wouldn't let in the pre-booked cowgirl stripper because there was a dress code that stipulated no denim. Fed up, the lads headed back to the Rovers, where a maudlin Sharon Gaskell was knocking back tequila as if her life depended on it. Drunk and aggressive, she told a startled Maxine it was inevitable some tart like Natalie or Sally would end up stealing her man. She was finally dragged home by Rita, as the bemused stags looked on.

Eddie Yeats, 1983

Eddie and fiancée Marion Willis wanted to keep news of Marion's pregnancy secret until after they were married, but interfering oaf Fred Gee got wind of it and announced it to the pub during the bin man's stag night. As Eddie tried to stop him, Fred punched him to the floor – and the next day Eddie turned up in church sporting a black eye!

Sunita Parekh, 2003

Sunita's Hindu hen-do was a riot of samosas, henna tattoos, fertility coconuts (which Bev accidentally sat on) and Bollywood dancing as Karen, Shelley, Janice and Deirdre did their best to shake their booty. Dev tried to dissuade Sunita from marrying Irish chef Ciaran McCarthy but she insisted she loved him. However, in the end the nuptials were cancelled when Sunita realised Ciaran had cold feet.

Ciaran: *'We're a great couple, me and Sunita – a good boyfriend and girlfriend – I'm just not too sure about the husband and wife. We've got fundamentally different attitudes.'*

Tracy: *'What attitudes?'*

Ciaran: *'She loves the idea of getting married, and I'd rather get run over by a bus.'*

Leanne Battersby, 2010

Stepmum Janice plus Eileen, Rita, Maria, Carla, Julie and
Deirdre were among the revellers as Leanne's hen party got
under way in the Rovers. Her ex Nick turned up and tried
one last time to get his former wife to run away with him.
Although she admitted to having doubts about marrying
Peter, she turned down his offer. Suddenly a huge explosion
tore through the Joinery and the residents watched in
horror as a tram smashed into the street from the viaduct
above. No one was more distraught than Leanne, who knew
Peter had been in there celebrating his stag do. However,
unlike Ashley Peacock, who perished in the devastating blast,
Peter was rescued and was rushed to intensive care, where
he married Leanne in a moving hospital bedside ceremony.

Dr Carter: *'Did I pick
the wrong night for
a quiet drink after
surgery?'*
Tina: *'I'd say you've
got an hour before
they start dancing
on the tables.'*

Roy Cropper, 1999

Forced into a stag night he didn't
want, Roy was then coerced into
forgoing his usual tomato juice for
something a little bit stronger. He
ended up so sozzled that Spider
and Curly had to carry him home
and Hayley was furious at them for
plying him with booze. However,
it turned out lightweight Roy had
only managed two pints!

Wedding Dos

Becky & Steve McDonald, 2009

Their first wedding day had been ruined because Becky was so sloshed they couldn't go ahead with the service. The couple's second attempt seemingly went without a hitch, but just as everyone was breathing a sigh of relief, things went horribly awry. Lloyd had just delivered his best man's speech when the police poured into the Rovers brandishing a warrant to search the premises. Everyone was stunned when a wad of drugs was found in Becky's handbag. It had been planted there by her ex, Slug, who had been paid by Becky's nemesis DC Hooch to stitch her up. She was hauled off to a prison cell where she spent a tearful night, whilst dressed in her wedding finery and pleading her innocence.

'She's come from the streets and that's where she belongs.'

Liz on Becky

205

'I was so sure me and Brian were going to live happily ever after, like in the fairy tales. Makes you glad you can't see what's ahead of you, don't it? If you did, you'd do away with yourself...'

Gail

Gail & Martin Platt, 1991

Everyone was in the mood to celebrate Gail and Martin's happy union apart from Gail's former mother-in-law, Ivy Brennan, who was just in a mood. She had plenty to moan about – the service had been in a registry office rather than a church, where was the wedding ring her son Brian had given Gail, and when little Nicky referred to Martin as his dad she totally lost it. 'Yer dad?' she snapped. 'Martin, you mean. Martin's not yer real dad, Nicky ... your real dad's in heaven,' she added, morosely. Bet and Gail were also getting nostalgic for the past as they reminisced about her wedding reception to Brian back in the Rovers in 1979. 'Of course you were only a kid then, the original child bride...' smiled the landlady before giving Gail a reassuring hug.

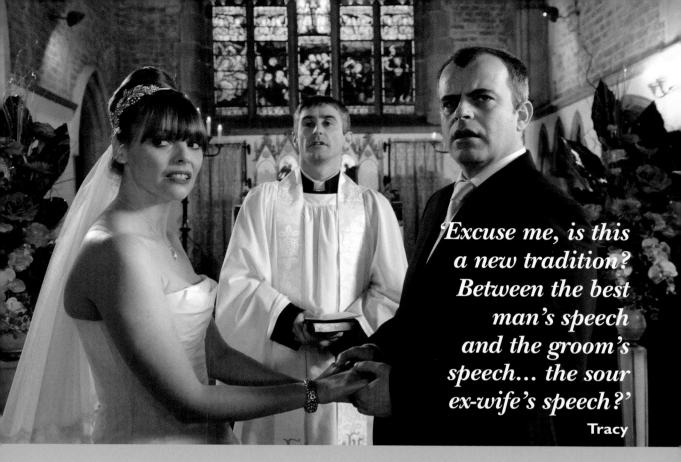

'Excuse me, is this a new tradition? Between the best man's speech and the groom's speech... the sour ex-wife's speech?'

Tracy

Tracy & Steve McDonald, 2012

Becky gatecrashed Tracy and ex-hubby Steve's big day armed with proof the schemer had lied about Becky killing her unborn babies. Instead of revealing the shocking truth there and then, she decided to let the ceremony go ahead, believing Steve and Tracy deserved each other after the way they'd treated her.

It was only after they'd tied the knot and everyone was at the Rovers' reception that Becky exacted her revenge and exposed Tracy's deceit. Handing an envelope to Steve containing Tracy's medical records, Becky explained to the whole pub: 'When she fell down my stairs – and that's "fell", folks, not "pushed" – there were no babies. Whatever she's been through, and trust me, I would not wish that on my worst enemy – which she is, by the way – it was nothing to do with me. She'd already lost the babies, Steve. Check the dates. Your shiny new wife's a filthy liar.'

She also made sure Deirdre's part in covering up Tracy's deception became common knowledge when she turned to Ken. 'She knew. Isn't that right, Dreary? Filthy liars – they run in the family.' Having cleared her name, Becky decided it was time to leave Weatherfield, and despite Steve's pleas she left to start a new life in Barbados with hunky hotelier Danny Stratton.

'Interesting speech, son, but I think you left somebody out. I'll give you a clue – 18 hours of agonising labour. Ring any bells?'

Jackie

Molly & Tyrone Dobbs, 2009

Gathered in front of a delighted Rovers' crowd, Tyrone was deliriously happy and couldn't wipe the smile off his face as he thanked everyone in his life: Jack, who'd been like a dad to him, Auntie Pam, Kevin, and most of all his beautiful wife, Mrs Molly Dobbs. He finished his speech by saying he knew he hadn't done too well family wise, but he had the best mates in the world. All this was watched by a grim-faced uninvited guest, his mother Jackie, who loudly moaned about being left out. In retaliation Tyrone was quick to remind her she'd previously stolen their wedding kitty money. Later, when no one was looking, Jackie pocketed the happy couple's wedding present – two Eurostar tickets – and sneaked out into the night.

Shelley Unwin, 2005

After dramatically ditching bully boy fiancé Charlie Stubbs at the altar, Shelley was reunited with her relieved mum outside the Rovers. Bev suggested she might want to avoid the crowd assembled inside for the wedding reception, but Shelley was determined to celebrate. 'She's back everyone, Shelley's back!' announced Bev, to enormous cheers from her concerned friends. Having been forced onto a diet by manipulative Charlie, Shelley only had eyes for the wedding cake. 'Right,' she declared, 'I'm going to cut that cake.' She helped herself to a huge slice, savoured her first delicious mouthful and looked happier than she had been for months. 'That ... is bloody gorgeous!' she announced with relish.

Deaths

'She weren't the biggest comedian we've ever had round 'ere, but she was good company for me.'
Ena on Martha

Martha Longhurst, 1964

In the middle of the snug sat three old ladies forever craning their necks to get the details on the latest pub tittle-tattle – hair-netted battle-axe Ena Sharples, timid cat-lover Minnie Caldwell and waspish gossip Martha Longhurst, who seemed to thrive on the misfortunes of others.

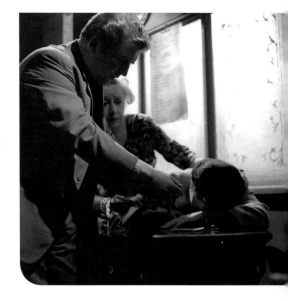

Supping their milk stout and huddled around their regular table in the ladies-only corner, the trio's conversation consisted of scandal (more often than not involving Elsie Tanner), ramblings from Minnie about Bobby the cat (which were often ignored by the others) and grim reaper Ena putting the world to rights. Despite the constant bickering between themselves the friends were inseparable, but tragic events in 1964 turned their world upside down.

There was a party atmosphere in the pub as Frank Barlow celebrated the sale of his shop, but while Ena led a singalong at the piano, Martha was feeling out of sorts and, unnoticed

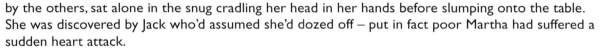

by the others, sat alone in the snug cradling her head in her hands before slumping onto the table. She was discovered by Jack who'd assumed she'd dozed off – put in fact poor Martha had suffered a sudden heart attack.

Martha may have gone, but she wasn't forgotten, and eleven years after her death barmaid Betty became convinced her ghost was haunting the premises after hearing her voice echoing around the snug. When Ena revealed she'd also seen Martha's ghost, some of the neighbours tried to contact the former regular through a ouija board. When what appeared to be Martha's spectacles were found on the bar, even Annie got the shivers, but much to everyone's relief the spooky mystery was solved when a customer turned up to claim them.

Edna Miller, 2001

All four of glum-faced Edna's previous landlords had dropped dead and she became convinced Duggie Ferguson would be next. When Duggie was away for the night, barmaid Shelley allowed Edna to stay for a boozy lock-in. But the next day Edna was nowhere to be seen, and when Duggie headed upstairs for a mid-afternoon nap, he got the shock of his life. There was Edna in his bed – dead! 'I should've seen it coming,' he later shuddered, alluding to Edna's doom-laden predictions. 'Oh, give over, it was all a load of mumbo-jumbo,' tutted Betty. Sunita agreed: 'She were about as psychic as one of Betty's hotpots!'

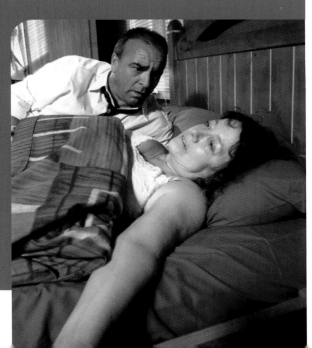

Ray Langton, 2005

Terminally ill with stomach cancer, Ray returned to Weatherfield after an absence of 27 years to make amends with his daughter Tracy. While Tracy was initially furious with her father for abandoning her, she began to soften, as did his former mother-in-law, Blanche: 'You know I've never liked you, Ray, but I'm glad that you've finally faced your responsibilities and made your peace with Tracy. You're not such a bad 'un after all…' During Ken and Deirdre's wedding reception he died alone in a booth. 'Not now, not yet. Ray … Dad,' sobbed Tracy, as she held him in her arms.

Eric Babbage, 2013

Holidaying Gloria thought her ship had come in when she met wealthy carpet king and businessman Eric, and she couldn't wait to flaunt her new loaded status on their return to Weatherfield. However, Eric was in fact drawn to Gloria's glamorous granddaughter Eva and he quietly admitted he'd rather take her on his world travels than marry money-grabbing Gloria. Just a few days later, he died suddenly in the Rovers' bar. Gloria's hopes of a huge windfall also died when estranged wife Doris turned up. She revealed she was his rightful heir, bitched about Eric's stinginess and gleefully informed a despondent Gloria she couldn't wait to spend his entire fortune. 'That man could squeeze a pound coin until the Queen's eyes bled,' she reminisced. However, three months later it emerged Eric had made a second will and Gloria had inherited a whopping £80,000 after all. She reluctantly parted with her cash to help fund the Rovers' renovations.

> *'You call that grieving? What if she finds out she's not in the will? Then you'll see what grieving is.'*
>
> **Eva on bereft Gloria**

Toni Griffiths, 2013

Off-duty firefighter Toni was overseeing a *Full Monty* charity show at the Bistro when a blaze took hold of the Rovers. She heroically rescued warped fire-starter Karl Munro from the inferno, but lost her own life when the first floor collapsed. Sunita Alahan was also trapped in the building and, despite being pulled to safety, later died in hospital.

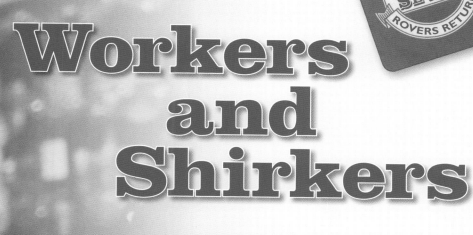
Workers and Shirkers

'**S**o the traveller's tales were right, you're not extinct – you and the abominable snowman!' snapped Bet to Fred Gee who'd been skiving in the cellar. For every Hilda Ogden-style grafter amongst the Rovers' workforce, there have always been the idlers who'd rather be supping the ale than serving it. From Fred to Karl Munro, Hilda to Harry Flagg, the Rovers wouldn't be the same without its motley mix of cleaners and pot-men...

The Cleaners

Martha Longhurst
1963–1964

Shortly after becoming the pub's cleaner, busybody pensioner Martha was taken on in a similar capacity at the Viaduct Street Social Club. But she struggled to cope with two jobs, and jumped at an invitation to go abroad for the first time to see her family. On the day Martha finally got her hands on her very first passport, she died of a heart attack in the Rovers' snug (see page 211).

Clara Midgeley
1966

Lonely pensioner Clara helped out for a couple of months, covering for Hilda, and set her sights on the gruff Albert Tatlock. The unlikely pair holidayed together in Cleveleys, but Albert did his best to avoid her on their return. Clara was both lovestruck and determined, and proposed to him. He declined, insisting he was too set in his ways to ever settle down again. When Hilda returned, heartbroken Clara realised there was no reason for her to stay in Weatherfield.

Hilda Ogden

1964–1987

When Annie reluctantly took on barmaid Irma's mother, Hilda, as her cleaner no one could have predicted that 23 years later she'd still be there, in her pinny and head-scarfed curlers, scrubbing the bar-top, warbling and gossiping away. However Hilda nearly didn't even make it through the first few months, because early on she was accused of stashing 12 bags of dodgy onions in the cellar to help her wheeler-dealer teenage son, Trevor.

Annie caught the family red-handed, but when the irate landlady threatened Trevor with a good hiding, Hilda flipped and was promptly dismissed alongside her daughter Irma. 'That suits me fine, you jumped-up old bat,' she snapped, and marched out of the pub. Luckily for Hilda, landlord Jack saw the funny side and reinstated her.

Hilda knew better than anyone that her husband Stan was a work-shy lump, and behind the closed doors of Number 13 she had no hesitation in pointing out his shortcomings, but woe betide anyone who dared have a go at him or any of her brood in public. While window-cleaner Stan's idea of hard labour was working up a thirst in the Rovers, Hilda was a grafter who at one point held down five jobs. But whether she was flitting between the factory, helping Stan out on his round or working as the cloakroom assistant at the Graffiti Club, it was the Rovers that remained a constant in Hilda's life, despite a fractious relationship with her employer Annie.

In 1977, when she was threatened with the sack for being too hung over to work, she sent Stan round to the pub to stand in for her. However Annie was aghast when Stan went out of his way to offend the customers, whilst smearing the tables with a floor cloth, and so she sent him packing. Hilda, of course, defended Stan's cleaning abilities. 'He's a professional, he's a window cleaner, in fact we are a family of professional cleaners, which puts us higher up in godliness than some folk I could name,' she sniffed at Annie, before storming back round to Number 13 to give Stanley what for after realising he'd stolen a pound from her wages.

> *'We are a family of professional cleaners, which puts us higher up in godliness than some folk I could name.'*
>
> **Hilda to Annie**

'Mrs Ogden has just walked into the living room grinning like an idiot and muttering, "Ignorance is bliss." If that were the case, of course, she'd be the happiest woman in the world.'

Annie on Hilda

Harry Flagg
2002–2004

Supping his pint in the Rovers, nice guy Harry was less than impressed with the murky gleam of the glasses and the state of the Gents. He revealed to a bemused Fred and Shelley that he'd worked as a cleaner at Manchester Airport for 20 years, with his remit including the VIP lavatories. 'That's when you realise a royal flush isn't just summut you get in a card game,' he informed them. Fred offered Harry £10 plus all the beer he could drink if he'd clean the Gents there and then, and after a thorough inspection, Fred declared the loos spotless and took him on full-time, combining both cleaning and pot-man duties.

However, Harry began to want more from life than mops and buckets, and decided to travel around Europe in the Croppers' camper van. Admitting he'd always had feelings for her, he asked Eileen Grimshaw to join him on his adventure, but she politely turned him down.

> *'To me, clean is classy. A decent pub should have a shine to it. Polished woodwork, gleaming brass, sparkling ale.'*
>
> **Harry to Fred**

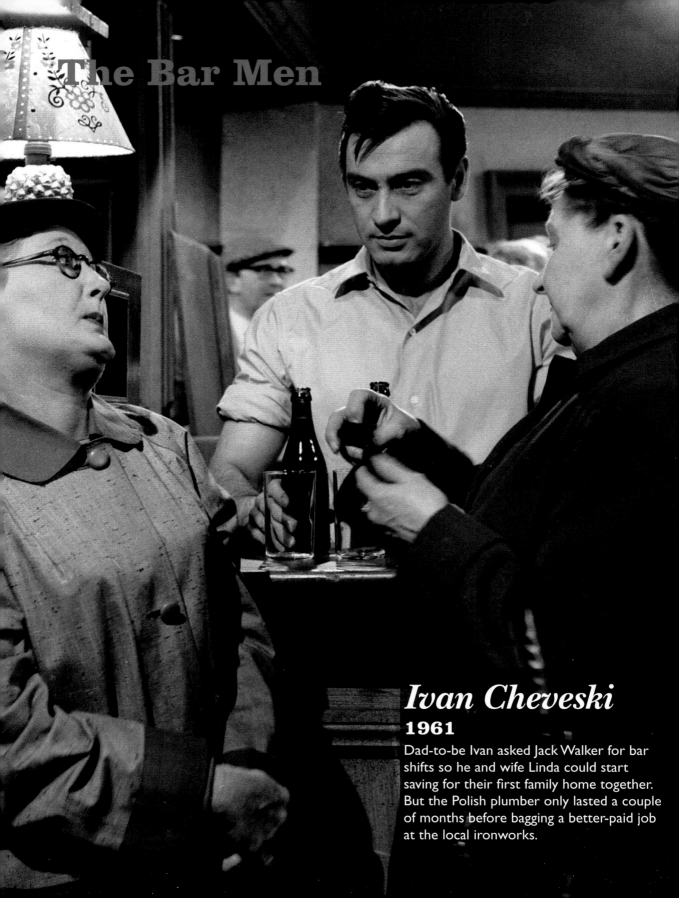

Ivan Cheveski

1961

Dad-to-be Ivan asked Jack Walker for bar shifts so he and wife Linda could start saving for their first family home together. But the Polish plumber only lasted a couple of months before bagging a better-paid job at the local ironworks.

Sam Leach
1962

When a tramp turned up at the Rovers no one was more surprised than builder Jerry Booth, who recognised the dishevelled old man as his Uncle Sam. The Walkers took Sam under their wing as pot-man, while Jerry tried to fathom how his uncle had ended up homeless. When the police turned up the regulars speculated he'd killed his wife Maureen, but it turned out he'd only left her and the police were after him for desertion.

Jacko Ford
1972

Corner-shop assistant Norma persuaded a reluctant Annie to take on her ex-con dad as pot-man, but Billy Walker was unconvinced and laid a trap for him by planting £3 next to the phone. Jacko quit in disgust but later agreed to return at Annie's request.

Eddie Yeats
1982

With Fred Gee laid up after falling down the cellar steps, ale-loving bin-man Eddie swapped sides of the bar and covered as pot-man for one week only.

Fred Gee
1976–1984

Oafish cellar-man Fred was full of his own self-importance and liked to think of himself as the alpha male of the pub. But in reality it was Annie who wore the trousers, while barmaids Bet and Betty tended to either ignore him or ridicule him.

They didn't know where to look when in 1979 he suddenly appeared behind the bar wearing a hairpiece. 'It doesn't suit you, Fred,' laughed regular Bert Tilsley. 'For a start off your hair looks 20 but your face looks 50!' When Albert Tatlock told him he looked daft, Annie intervened by sticking up for Fred. 'Everyone is entitled to make the best of themselves,' she decreed. 'Although in your case, Fred, I'm not sure you've succeeded...'

Fed up of being Annie's dogsbody and chauffeur, Fred had his sights on running his own pub. The brewery offered him the tenancy of the Mechanics on Commercial Road, but said he would need to find a wife first. He attempted to butter up both Betty and Bet with marriage proposals but they both turned him down flat, and after a few disastrous dates he shelved his landlord ambitions.

In 1984 Newton & Ridley gave him an opportunity to shine when they temporarily put him in charge of the Rovers. He revelled in lording it over Bet and Betty, sticking a sign behind the bar announcing himself as the watering hole's new host. 'Oi, what's that's supposed to be?' asked Betty. 'That, Betty, is an omen of change,' Fred declared pompously, in his bow tie and blazer. 'That is a reminder to the humble punter that his host has his interests at heart, it's a sign that the slipshod slap-happy days in this boozer are well and truly over.' Ignoring him, Bet continued filing her nails. 'That big fat slob's not going to ruin my life without a scrap,' she muttered to Betty, who nodded in agreement.

Fred's reign was cut short when he was struck down with pneumonia and on his return he found a brusque Billy Walker in charge – who promptly gave Fred a week's notice. After an argument about severance pay, Fred thumped Billy, thereby ending his Rovers' career.

> ## 'That big fat slob's not going to ruin my life without a scrap.'
>
> **Bet on temporary manager Fred**

Wilf Starkey
1985

The know-it-all pot-man ended up in hot water when he pocketed an envelope containing £4,000 belonging to factory boss Mike Baldwin. He handed it back to Bet and broke down, admitting he'd never done anything like that before. She gave him a second chance but when the till was £5 short, he felt Bet thought he was the culprit, so he resigned. Ken turned up with the missing £5 saying he'd been given too much change, but Bet's apologies came too late and Wilf already had another job.

Frank Mills
1985–1986

Bet met barman Frank in Blackpool and a few weeks later he turned up at the Rovers. She took him on and put him up in the spare room, but he wanted more from Bet and, after convincing her he was sticking around, they spent the night together. Within days he'd accepted a job on a Norwegian cruise liner – leaving Bet angry and feeling used. He returned a month later, but became aggressive when barmaid Gloria Todd rejected his advances, so Bet told him to sling his hook.

Jack Duckworth
1985, 1986–1995, 1999

With his spectacles held together with sticking-plaster, loveable rogue and hen-pecked hubby Jack Duckworth was in his element supping in the Rovers' bar. So when he was given his first trial as cellar-man by Bet, he was overjoyed. But he was furious when wife Vera started mouthing off at him in the pub and lost him the only job he'd ever enjoyed.

All Vera wanted was for Jack to go back to his window-cleaning round, but he wasn't going to give up on pub life that easily. After a word with George Newton at the brewery, Bet was persuaded to reinstate him and for the next decade he was the pub's amiable pot-man until he took over landlord duties in 1995.

In 1989 Jack walked out when an accusatory Bet told him the till was down, but he later admitted to Vera he'd been giving people the wrong change because his eyesight was going. 'My eyesight's bad, me hair's falling out, me teeth are going. I'm not as randy as I was. I've even got athlete's foot,' he sighed. 'I'm tellin' ya, Vee, I'm crackin' up. Your old man is near enough ready for the knacker's yard!'

But Jack still had a wandering eye and he made a play for bubbly barmaid Tina Fowler, who shocked him by agreeing to a date. He wined and dined Tina at an expensive restaurant, but when he tried to kiss her, she told him she'd only wanted a meal and to add insult to injury he ran out of petrol on the way home.

Vera found the restaurant receipt in his jacket pocket and suspected he was seeing someone behind her back, but when she sneered that no woman in her right mind would be interested in him, Jack snapped and told her about his night out with Tina. Needless to say, Vera flipped and tackled Tina in the pub, throwing a pint at her, but she ducked and Alec was drenched instead. He barred Vera who stormed home and took her revenge by cutting up all Jack's trousers.

After his stint as landlord flopped due to the Duckworths' inability to balance the books, Jack soon found himself back on pot-man duties, this time with Natalie Barnes in charge. He was diagnosed with a heart condition, but determined to keep on working, he had Vera secretly help him lug crates up from the cellar. However, after a heart attack and a bypass operation, Jack knew his days at the Rovers were numbered. He was presented with a tankard as his leaving gift and soon adapted to life propping up the bar from the other side – with a pint in his hand!

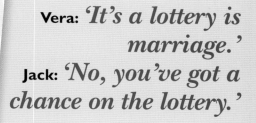

Vera: *'It's a lottery is marriage.'*
Jack: *'No, you've got a chance on the lottery.'*

233

Charlie Bracewell

1989

A former ventriloquist on Alec's showbiz-agent books, down-on-his-luck Charlie was taken on because Alec felt sorry for him. His favourite topic of conversation seemed to be death, but on a brighter note he also took a fancy to Betty. Initially charmed by him, she was soon demanding he leave after he pinched her bottom. While Alec couldn't bring himself to ditch his chum, Bet hatched a plan to get rid of Charlie by offloading him onto rival landlady Stella Rigby at the White Swan.

Andy McDonald

1994–1997

When celebrating his acceptance onto a Combined Studies course at Manchester University, Andy mentioned to Bet that he was looking for part-time bar work. She immediately took him on and got him clearing away the empties, much to barmaid Raquel's consternation as she'd intended to ask Bet to take on recently sacked supermarket manager, Curly Watts.

Spider Nugent

1999

Short-staffed new landlady Natalie persuaded eco-warrior Spider to help out behind the bar, much to the disgust of fellow employee Vera who sniped: 'We don't have riff-raff like you behind the bar – go on sling yer hook!' But Natalie was adamant that Spider stayed and promptly demoted former licensees Jack and Vera to more menial positions. Believing he was doing the Duckworths out of a job, Spider quit as a matter of principle a mere 24 hours after being taken on full-time.

Bill Webster
1995

On being dumped by his wife Elaine, Kevin's dad turned up in Weatherfield and kipped down on the sofa at Number 13. Space was tight in the tiny terrace and it was a relief when Bet took him on as the Rovers' live-in pot-man. But Bill lost his job a few weeks later when the Duckworths took over as licensees.

Sandy Hunter
1998

After an afternoon on the port and lemon at the Coach & Horses, landlady Vera Duckworth staggered in and announced she'd solved their staffing problem by poaching one of the rival pub's workers. 'A right cracker, blond, good-looking,' she informed a drooling Alec and Jack. When their new employee turned out to be a he and not a she, and a young, hunky, handsome one at that, the crestfallen pair wanted rid of him.

But Vera was adamant Sandy was staying and he even created a new cocktail, naming it in honour of his employer, 'Ere, have a sip of this, Jack. It's lovely, a Bloody Vera,' she swooned.

'No thanks,' he replied. 'I've 'ad enough of them to last me a lifetime.'

Meanwhile Alec spotted Sandy's smooth way with the ladies and secretly signed him up to work as an escort with his Golden Years Agency. When Vera discovered her precious protégé was moonlighting while supposedly off sick, she called him a traitor and sacked him on the spot.

Martin Platt
1999

Martin lost his job at the hospital thanks to compo-seeking patient Les Battersby who'd falsely accused Martin of negligence, so the unemployed nurse offered his services at the pub. Wife Gail was appalled by their obvious decline in status, but luckily she only had to endure a week of Martin being behind the bar before he found a job as assistant manager at an old people's home.

Vinny Sorrell
1999–2000

There was an instant chemistry between the former Nuttalls' brewery drayman and Natalie, but as the pair went public with their relationship, a power struggle developed behind the bar. While Vinny wanted them to work as a team, Natalie never failed to remind him who was boss. Fed up of being treated like her lackey, Vinny cleared his stuff out of the Rovers and bedded her younger sister Debs. Natalie was devastated by their betrayal and the cheating pair quit Weatherfield to work on a cruise ship, with Vinny oblivious to the fact that Natalie was pregnant with his child.

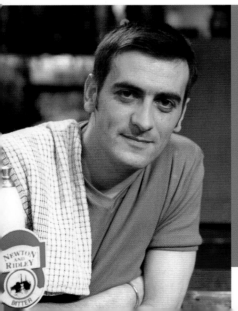

Peter Barlow
2001

Peter was delighted when landlord Duggie Ferguson showed him where all the spare bottles of spirits were stored and happily helped himself. A few days later barmaid Toyah Battersby caught him diluting the whisky with water, but he made her keep her mouth shut. The next day the trading standards inspectors made an unexpected appearance after a tip-off about the watered-down booze.

Peter encouraged Duggie's hunch it was Toyah who'd grassed and she was sacked. He later enjoyed another night of knocking back freebies after Duggie asked him to lock up, but his boss had set a trap by marking the bottle levels. When he was confronted Peter still refused to confess and Duggie chucked him out.

Ciaran McCarthy
2003–2005, 2010

Ciaran's twinkly-eyed Irish charm had most of the women of Weatherfield smiling. He was engaged to Sunita but ended up drunkenly spending the night with Shelley's mum Bev. When he ignored her further attempts at seduction, she sacked him. Owner Fred Elliott, recognising that being fired for refusing sexual advances was a case of unfair dismissal, quickly reinstated him.

Even his boss Liz McDonald took a fancy to him, but Ciaran only had eyes for fellow bar-worker Michelle Connor. He persuaded her to let him cook a meal on their date to prove what an incredible chef he was. But he failed to get to grips with Michelle's oven, burned the chicken and dished up beans on toast instead. She had issued him with a forfeit should he fail to impress and he kept his word by serving behind the bar wearing only his boxer shorts. 'If this is going to be a regular thing we're never going to be out of this place,' gawped machinist Fiz Stape.

'Once word of this gets around there's going to be women queuing around the block to get in here,' he smirked. Michelle rolled her eyes. 'Ooh, modest as ever.' But the smile was soon wiped off Ciaran's face when Janice Battersby lurched for him. 'Well, if you ask me I think you're a tad overdressed,' she growled. 'Come on, cutie pie – let's see what you're really made of...' as she chased a terrified Ciaran.

Vernon Tomlin

2006–2008

There was an instant attraction between the work-shy musician and Rovers' manager Liz McDonald when Vernon's band the Rocky Rhythm Rascals played at the Weatherfield Traders Association Christmas dinner. The loved-up pair began dating and Liz even inspired Vernon to write a song about her. 'Your "her" goes next to my "his". You make my heart go like Billy Whizz. You're every answer in my pub quiz. You are my Liz, you are my Liz...' But Steve was less than impressed. 'Did you get a three-year-old to write that?' he asked.

When Michelle, a vocalist in Vernon's band, started working at the Rovers, Liz was convinced she had the hots for her boyfriend. But it was a lecherous Vernon who was pestering the new barmaid for some quality time together, so Michelle decided to teach him a lesson.

She phoned him on his mobile one night saying she was in the back room of the Rovers and ready for him. Vernon bounded into the room wearing nothing but leopard-skin undies and lunged at her, crooning, 'I'm ready now, I'm ready now...' He stopped in his tracks when he spotted Betty and Sean perched on the sofa. 'I don't know what you're ready for, but it's nothing that I'd be interested in!' quipped Betty, and the trio fell about guffawing.

When Liz found out what'd been going on she threw all of his belongings (including his beloved drum-kit) out of the Rovers' upstairs window and sent him packing. Vernon begged her for a second chance and the couple finally married in 2007, even though Vernon had been beaten up by Liz's jealous ex Jim on the morning of their wedding. Liz soon regretted marrying him and they split the following year.

'What could possibly be better in Vernon's world? He's got a girlfriend who owns a pub!'

Lloyd

Lewis Archer

2012

Hairdresser Audrey Roberts was surprised to walk into the Rovers and find boyfriend Lewis offering her a gin and tonic from behind the bar. Barmaid Gloria Price informed her he'd come highly recommended by her grandson. 'Not that one,' she added, nodding at a snarling David. 'The nice one.' She went on to gush that Lewis was a natural who could charm the birds from the trees.

He was later shocked when a sobbing Gloria revealed she was dying. He provided a sympathetic ear and as the pair became closer, she begged Lewis to move to Spain with her, promising to leave everything to him in her will.

It turned out that her life-threatening illness was all part of a scam cooked up by Audrey's daughter Gail McIntyre to prove he was still a money-grabbing hustler. He wasn't, and had turned Gloria down, but when he discovered Audrey had known about the scheming, he felt betrayed and decided that he had no choice but to end their relationship. He got his revenge on Gloria by exposing her as a cheat in the Pub of the Year competition. His payback for Gail was a much more elaborate affair – convincing her that he was in love with her and that they should run off to Italy together, before stealing £40,000 from her bank account and disappearing.

'Locked in a pub cellar? You dream about summut like this happening to you.'

Albert's fantasy comes true

Going Underground

The dingy cellar has seen a few unexpected guests over the years...

1976

When Stan Ogden and Albert Tatlock offered to change a barrel for Bet, they ended up being locked in the cellar overnight. The pair panicked until it occurred to them they were surrounded by barrels of their beloved beer and so they proceeded to get blind drunk. 'Fancy a milk stout for starters?' grinned Albert. After the brewery heard of their exploits, they insisted Annie hire a cellar-man to ensure this kind of debacle never happened again.

1982

Portly pot-man Fred Gee fell down the creaking stairs and threatened to sue, claiming he'd injured his back. Determined to find out if he was faking it, Annie arranged for a physiotherapist to give him the once over. But instead of a soothing rub-down by a curvy masseuse, Fred found himself being pummelled by burly rugby club physio Nipper Harris – who confirmed there was absolutely nothing wrong with him.

1996

Awoken in the middle of the night by strange noises coming from the cellar, a spooked Jack and Vera were convinced it was the ghost of Ivy Brennan trying to make her presence heard. Instead they found ghost-busting Roy Cropper camping out in there. 'Are you a medium?' asked a relieved Vera. 'No, I'm a 42,' he replied.

2008

Convinced that bookie Dan Mason had scratched his car, Steve McDonald reacted childishly by chucking Dan's mobile into the cellar. The pair tussled and when Dan went in after his phone, Steve locked him down there, turned off the lights and went to bed. Unbeknownst to Steve, Dan had injured himself and was rushed to hospital the next day with a ruptured spleen. Steve was arrested for assault and unlawful imprisonment, but Dan later agreed to drop the charges.

♀ At Your Convenience ♂

Sometimes the best Rovers' gossip happens behind closed doors...

In 1967 cleaner Hilda Ogden almost flooded the whole pub when she accidentally pulled a tap off a sink in the Ladies loos. The following year Albert Tatlock climbed out of the window in the Gents to escape the amorous attentions of his unwanted fiancée, Alice Pickins. Things hotted up in 2006 when Jamie Baldwin and his stepmother Frankie shared an illicit kiss and a year later, after the smoking ban came in, pensioner Blanche Hunt caught Liz McDonald having a crafty ciggie in a cubicle. In 2012 Michelle Connor was shocked to discover her wayward son Ryan taking drugs in there.

Tracy Barlow, however, always seems to find the conveniences of great convenience. She often takes her tinkle just when there's a row kicking off and of course gleefully uses the information to her own advantage. In 2006 she overheard Shelley and Bev Unwin rowing about Charlie Stubbs and in 2011 Leanne Barlow was appalled to discover Tracy had overheard her row with Carla Connor – during which she'd admitted to her affair with Nick Tilsley!

LADIES

You dirty little filth monger ... you ought to be ashamed of yourself!

Showtime

In the days before *Britain's Got Talent* and *The X Factor* the Rovers Return was the place to be entertained. Who can forget Jack's crooning (some called it caterwauling), Rita's soaring vocals, Norris's knack for drag and perhaps most bizarre of all Percy Sugden's farmyard impressions (which failed to wow the crowd). The hidden talents of the Street's regulars means showtime at the Rovers is always a night to remember...

That's Entertainment!
1969

Jittery organisers Emily and Ernest were convinced that no one was going to turn up for the festive talent show, but they needn't have worried, the event was a roaring success. Accompanied by Len on drums, Ken had the crowd humming along as he tooted 'Edelweiss' on his trumpet, and a nervous Minnie kept everyone entertained with her rendition of 'The Owl and the Pussycat' – even though she managed to forget the lyrics after the first verse.

Irma was a hit as Lancashire comedienne Hylda Baker, but hapless Bernard Butler wasn't a natural performer as her sidekick Cynthia; tottering in his heels he managed to fall over while both getting on and off the stage. Meanwhile, Albert was late as he'd superglued on a beard for an earlier stint as Father Christmas and hadn't been able to get it off. Arriving in the bar with the beard still attached he screamed in agony when Stan yanked it off without any warning!

Another Fine Mess?

1973

After losing a bowling match against the men, the forfeit handed out to the women was to produce a cabaret show … in drag! Emily was master of ceremonies sporting a big swirly moustache, Norma did her best Ken Dodd impersonation and Bet and Betty were an uncanny Laurel and Hardy. But professional chanteuse Rita Littlewood wasn't dressing down for anyone and swanned onto the stage decked out in a glamorous blonde wig, feather boa and a sparkly pink frock as female drag act Danny La Rue – which led to Ray booing and calling for her to be disqualified.

Forties' Frolics

1972

The boozed-up Christmas Day crowd had already cheered on Bet, Betty and Norma Ford as the harmonising Andrews Sisters, Rita as a dulcet-toned Marlene Dietrich, Alf and Ernest as the monocled Western Brothers and landlady Annie patriotically dressed as Britannia and warbling 'There'll Always Be an England'. So by the time Master of Ceremonies Billy announced Emily as the 'sensational closing act', the audience had high hopes for a grand finale. But just as a sheepish Emily shuffled onstage dressed as Carmen Miranda, a couple of bananas fell from the pile of fruit precariously balanced on her head. The regulars roared with laughter as she spluttered an apology and promptly disappeared backstage again.

'I'm sorry we haven't got any
dancing girls this year; Mrs Caldwell
and Mrs Sharples were booked to
appear but they hadn't got their
grass skirts ready in time...'

Billy

Acting Up
1974

It was Emily and Ernest who came up with the idea of the Rovers' Amateur Dramatic Association (RADA), and after falling out over the borderline pornographic new play that Ernest initially wanted to stage, the pair finally settled on Emily's choice, *The Importance of Being Earnest*. But when her husband's dictatorial leadership style was challenged by the cast (Rita had already walked out after some particularly cutting criticism), Emily took over as director, much to everyone's delight.

The show – staged at the Community Centre across the street – was a huge success despite Annie (as Lady Bracknell) ruining the dress she'd hired from a theatrical costumier by sitting on a freshly painted piece of scenery. Meanwhile, stage-hand Mavis had the shock of her life when she stumbled into the men's dressing room by mistake and was confronted by a stark-naked Billy Walker!

The Importance of Being Earnest

Lady Bracknell	Annie Walker
Algernon	Ken Barlow
Jack	Jerry Booth
Cecily	Bet Lynch
Gwendolen	Deirdre Hunt
Lane	Len Fairclough
Miss Prism	Emily Bishop
Canon Chasuble	Ernest Bishop
Masters	Billy Walker
Directed by	Emily Bishop

Let Us Entertain You!

1984

To her horror Mavis was nominated as the organiser of the Pub Olympics' evening entertainment, and after much discussion by the committee it was decided the event would be a talent contest. Predictably, Mavis was a bag of nerves, convinced the turns would be awful – and she wasn't far wrong! Alf's stand-up comedy routine was leaden and Percy's attempt at farmyard impersonations had to be seen to be believed. Luckily factory machinists Vera Duckworth and Ivy Tilsley were on hand to sing 'We're a Couple of Swells' dressed as tramps and steal the show.

> *'It's not easy being an impresario, you know, Mave. Ask Paul Raymond.'*
>
> **Bet**

254

The Cringe Factor

1986

Frustrated singer Jack reckoned he'd be catapulted to stardom by crooning a couple of numbers at the open-mic night. But Bet had other ideas. 'The only number I want from you is the one you're getting paid for — behind the bar and down't cellar,' she informed the crestfallen pot-man. But refusing to give up on his dream, Jack donned

his medallion and best jacket for that night's shift on the off-chance the landlady had a change of heart.

Horrified at the regulars leaving in droves to avoid the off-key singers and drunk novelty acts, in desperation Bet allowed Jack his moment in the spotlight. But his singing was hopelessly out of tune and when Vera joined in caterwauling with him on 'The Lady Is a Tramp' they practically emptied the place!

Sing-a-longa Reg!

1995

In an attempt to impress Bet on her return from holiday, temporary manager Rodney Bostock organised a karaoke evening. At first Bet was horrified to be confronted by a hip-thrusting Reg Holdsworth belting out 'Rawhide', but she mellowed when a smitten Rodney told her he'd come up with the idea for her, not the brewery. Making herself comfortable on the bar, Bet joined in the fun by singing the appropriately titled 'Dancing in the Street'.

Weatherfield's Got Talent
1996

Or has it? Alec's talent night included novelty acts such as body-stockinged Melanie Power, who jiggled about whilst tearing a copy of the Yellow Pages, a jaw-droppingly awful mother-and-son mind-reading act called Shadow and Sun, hairdresser Maxine Peacock nervously warbling her way through 'Twist and Shout' and even Percy Sugden threatened to get on stage with his ukulele. Unable to watch from the sidelines any longer, wannabe crooner Jack started on 'My Way' (the third rendition of the night), but someone pulled the plug from the PA system!

Secret Stripper!

2000

Sam Kingston was a builder by day, but none of his workmates were aware that by night he performed as a stripper under the stage-name the Masked Python. When barmaid Geena recognised him by the tattoo on his arm he agreed to strut his stuff at a Rovers' 'women-only night' as he needed the cash. But when a drunken Janice Battersby lurched forward and pulled off his mask it was hard to tell who was more mortified – Sam or his furious mum, Brenda, who'd just happened to be in the pub!

'Just you wait 'til I get you home – showing off yer bits and pieces in front of a load of drunken women!'

Sam's mum Brenda

Life's a Drag

2001

'I don't believe it – the flippin' fancy dress shop has forgotten to give me any false boobs!' cried Duggie, as he prepared to transform himself into the hostess with the mostest. 'It's not the end of the world...' replied Steve, who was using rolled-up socks to create his cleavage. 'It is when you're Dolly Parton!' sighed Duggie.

A last-minute dash to the corner shop for balloons averted a flat-chested crisis, but Duggie had only been onstage a matter of minutes before his first boob popped, swiftly followed by the other one which deflated itself. Also appearing at the pop-star-themed drag night were the garage lads as girl group The Shangri-Las, Les rocking out as Suzi Quatro and Steve and Vik Desai camping it up as Agnetha and Frida on 'Dancing Queen'. But it was Norris as growly chanteuse Eartha Kitt, sporting a pair of Rita's best earrings, who was unanimously declared the winner by barmaid judges Shelley and Betty.

Shelley: *'We should do more of this stuff – it's a scream!'*

Betty: *'I'll be deaf before the night's out.'*

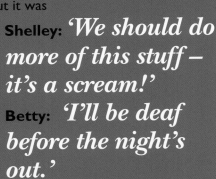

Soul sisters

2006

A smitten Steve couldn't take his eyes off Michelle Connor when she wowed the crowd at karaoke night, much to the annoyance of Liz, who'd taken against the singer from day one. 'At this rate we'll have to start a flamin' fan club for her...' she grimaced. Deciding to show Michelle how it was done, the landlady took to the stage with best mates Deirdre and Eileen and caterwauled her way through 'It's Raining Men'. The trio were followed by Sean who persuaded Jamie Baldwin to duet with him on 'Don't Go Breaking My Heart' – making Violet jealous because boyfriend Jamie had turned her down when she'd suggested they sing together.

Michelle: *'Get yourself down Canal Street on a Saturday night, you'll see hundreds of Liz lookalikes.'*
Sean: *'You saying she looks like a tranny?'*
Michelle: *'Your words, not mine.'*

It's Behind You!

2009

Steve discovered a box of faded panto photos from days gone by and while veteran barmaid Betty reminisced as she sifted through them, Becky and Claire Peacock decided to bring some festive cheer to the pub by staging their own charity production of *Cinderella*. The pair battled it out for the title role, but things got even rockier when a victorious Claire had to kiss Becky's hubby Steve, who was playing a rather wooden Prince Charming.

Kids' entertainer Jesse Chadwick and barman Sean were the Ugly Sisters, while hapless Graeme Proctor (Buttons) had to perform in crutches after falling off his window-cleaning ladder. When Cinders told a wand-waving Betty she didn't look much like a Fairy Godmother, Betty snapped back: 'Yes, well, Kylie Minogue was busy, now hurry up because I've got some hotpots in the oven.'

But it was little Amy Barlow who stole the show when she took to the stage to sing, froze and instead hissed 'bollocks' to gasps from the audience. 'Maybe they could give some of the money to the Tourette's trust?' suggested Eileen, with a grin.

Cinderella

Cinderella	Claire Peacock
Prince Charming	Steve McDonald
Buttons	Graeme Proctor
Dandini	Becky McDonald
Gorgonzola	Sean Tully
Carbunkula	Jesse Chadwick
Fairy Godmother	Betty Williams
Directed by	John Stape